Still Standing

Still Standing

**WHEN YOU HAVE EVERY REASON
TO GIVE UP, KEEP GOING**

■ ■ ■

Kevin Rempel

Dedication

■ ■ ■

THIS BOOK IS DEDICATED TO the three most important women in my life.

First to you, Mom. You have been beyond incredible through all you have been through. You never judged me for anything, you always supported me and travelled the world to come watch me play hockey. I'm so thankful to have a mother so caring in my life. You have truly taught me what unconditional love really is.

To my Groovy Granny, GG! You are unbelievable. I'm so thankful that I have a great relationship with my grandmother and you are continually a riot to be around. There's never a dull moment with you. Your energy is infectious and you make us laugh so much trying to keep up with you. Try and make it to 100, would ya?

To my sister bear, Rebecca! I'm so proud of you. Moving away to Australia and New Zealand to pursue your dreams makes me proud that you too haven't held back in life from fear, but chased after what means the most to you and you too haven't given up. You inspire me each time we talk and I can't wait to see what else you accomplish in your lifetime.

I love the three of you more than anything else in this world.

To Dad. I love you and I forgive you.

Acknowledgements

■ ■ ■

THERE ARE SO MANY OF you who have helped get me to where I am today I feel like I might leave someone out. Every person I've ever had the chance to speak with in a parking lot, from a podium, in a gymnasium, at the dirtbike track, a hockey rink, or drunk at a party, you have been a part of my journey. Thank you.

To my dearest friends:

Mike Koval and the Koval family, The Scott family, The Crawley's, Mudman and The Lind family, Bill Teggart, Ryan Goertz, Brian and Tina Johnson, Brock Thom, Ben Hage, Matt Doherty, David Izer and DMXS, Jason Lambert, Steve Churm, Rob King, Deanna Duquette, Chris MacPherson, Blair Bouchard, Joel and Linda McVea and my Dundas neighbours, Tim Krause, Josh Quail, Mikey Bolahood, and Forrest Willett.

To Les Kletke, and Kim Rempel. Thank you for helping me put my story on paper.

To my rehab team:

Marianne Lawton, Beverly Drakeford, Carolyn Hay, Joanne Smith, Chris Brownell, Mary Anderson, and Tracy Goertz.

To my trainers in sport:

McMaster University and staff at the David Braley Athletic Centre, Jeremy Steinbach, Ben Bahrami, Ted & Dan at BTNL, and Natascha Wesch.

To my hockey family:

Sport By Ability Niagara, Mississauga Cruisers, Elmvale Bears, Ontario Sledge Hockey Association players and staff, Hockey Canada, Mike Mondin, Billy McGuigan, Curtis Hunt, Adam Crockatt, Tony Carbonette, Jamie Kissick, Roch Dorion, Jan Antons, and all my teammates I played with over the years. Thank you for helping me become the best player I could be.

Preface

■ ■ ■

EVER SINCE THE DAY MY dad got injured I thought about writing a book. I thought my life was crazy then. As time progressed my story just kept getting bigger and bigger, not really slowing down.

Over the years people continually would say to me "You should write a book!". I thought that would be awesome, but not until I am done with hockey. At least "Not until I compete in the Paralympics", I would tell myself.

Fast forward to today. I have accomplished almost all of my goals and this was one of the big items to check off on the bucket list. I put my head down for 12 weeks and wrote my manuscript.

During the writing process there was a bit of cathartic value involved, but mostly I had a lot of fun. I enjoyed sharing stories that I would not normally speak about on stage. I often tell people that if you are to celebrate me for who I am today and why I am here, then this is what I want you to know. I want you to know the truth. The real nitty gritty of what went on behind the scenes.

This my friends, is the result.

Although my story will never be finished, I am thrilled to get this chapter of my life out there. When I leave this world, people will know my story and I have left a legacy behind for myself and my family. I am proud of that.

Someday I know I would like to write another book. Just like anything, after you do it once you know it will be easier to do it again. In the meantime, I hope that through sharing my story you find one thing that inspires you to carry on through your own challenges.

My friends, you are not alone in your struggles. We all have our own story.

Through reading mine I wish for you to live yours.

CHAPTER 1

Life Is About To Get Crazy

■ ■ ■

IT WAS DECEMBER 11, 2002, and Dad and I planned to go deer hunting and put a few hours in the tree stand before I had to go back to Niagara College and write my last exam for the semester. We left at 5:30am and were sitting quietly in our tree stands by 6:15am.

I stayed until 8:30am, and then had to leave for school. Dad stayed in his tree stand and continued hunting. When my exam was completed I called Dad.

"Hey, how did you make out? Did you see anything this morning?"

"I did!" Dad said, "I took a shot around 8:00am and the deer ran off."

"Awesome!" I said.

"Do you want to come back and help me track it down?" Dad asked.

"Absolutely. I'll see you shortly."

When I returned to our location I met Dad in the farmer's field where we parked our trucks. We whispered to each other, not wanting to scare off the deer in case the deer had only been wounded.

We made our way back to the tree stand, and searched for the blood trail. We found the first drops of blood, and followed the trail. After nearly 45 minutes (much longer than usual) we finally found the young buck resting peacefully in the woods. We field dressed him, and loaded him in the truck.

Finally Dad had gotten his first deer of the season. Little did we know it would be his last.

We returned home for lunch and took a quick nap before heading back out in the afternoon. Dad wanted to go back early to build a new tree stand in a prime area and hopefully nail a big one, so after a few short hours we were back at it again. We were only fifteen minutes into building the stand when the unthinkable happened. I had just finished passing Dad some material, and climbed back down the tree. Just as I took a step back I heard a branch snap. I looked up and in that split second I saw my dad fall twenty-five feet straight to the ground.

He laid there dazed and confused gasping for air. I asked him if he was alright but it was clear from the few words he could mutter out that he couldn't feel or move his legs. I quickly ran to get help.

I remembered in that moment always having wondered what it might feel like to run for your life. I'd always seen it in movies. Well, I wasn't running for my life but I was running for my dad's. My boots were heavy. I had multiple layers of clothes on, and I couldn't stop.

When I got to the truck I called 911. The ambulance, police cruisers, firefighters, and a helicopter, showed up to help get my Dad out. Even the TV news crew was there.

Right after I called 911, I called my mom too. She was out with a friend that night and had left her phone in the car. During dinner though, her dry hands had begun to hurt, so she walked out to her car to get hand cream. It was at that exact moment I happened to call. I told her what had happened to Dad and she headed straight to the hospital. Had it not been for her hands hurting just then, she would have never made it to the hospital in time to see the doctors before Dad's surgery.

As Mom and I arrived at the hospital, doctors had already taken x-rays and were confident about the diagnosis. Dad had fractured his fifth, sixth, and seventh vertebrae. They showed us the x-ray film. Instead of square blocks, Dad's vertebrae looked like piles of crushed diamonds. I am no doctor, but seeing that didn't give me much confidence.

I was into the Bible at the time and said a prayer beside the bed before Dad went into surgery. The doctors fused five of Dad's vertebrae together and he was deemed a complete paraplegic which meant he had no chance of ever walking again.

Back home our community was in shock. Everyone knew my dad. He'd worked for the Town of Lincoln for decades driving a backhoe and digging ditches. He was always on the streets saying hello to everyone. Everyone knew my dad, and poured out immense support.

Local contractors donated many hours of labor to help with renovating our house to make it wheelchair accessible. We priced out needed materials, and our next door neighbors started a fundraiser. Our community helped raise $20,000 for renovation materials.

We gutted my parents' bedroom to install an accessible shower. All the carpet was removed and laminate hardwood was laid to make wheeling around easier. Elevators were installed both outside and inside the house. While these things were all a huge help, everything was quite a whirlwind at the same time.

Dad had spent three months in Chedoke hospital in Hamilton and his return home was quickly approaching. I was still busy trying to complete college while working part time at bricklaying. Mom would leave work and go straight to the hospital to visit Dad, then have to sleep in the parking lot before she could drive home because she was so tired. Mom will tell you that there were times it was very dangerous for her driving home, trying to keep her eyes open.

She did everything she could to support and be there for him.

When Dad finally did come home, he was mad. The anger and resentment had built up over time in the hospital, but it got even worse once he returned home and experienced reality.

"Why is the closet so small? I wanted it bigger."

"This color looks stupid."

"Why does the elevator make that noise?"

It felt like he wasn't happy with anything, yet we had just done everything we could. That first day he came home we felt like a failure. I knew it wasn't true, but his reaction made us feel like nothing we did was right.

In addition to the shock of this new lifestyle, there was the added issue of his bowel and bladder. He had no control over those functions, so soiling himself became frequent. I would wake up often at 3:00am to the pungent odor wafting from across the hall. He would yell and scream and take out his frustration on Mom while she removed the sheets, cleaned the bed, and put on clean bedding. Then, after they went back to bed, Dad would sometimes soil the bed again just thirty minutes later.

Many nights I would lie awake wondering what was happening. Why did this happen? Why do I have to be the kid whose life is affected by my dad's injury?

Other nights Dad was below me in the basement watching TV and I could hear him crying. He would cry for hours, and when he finally did come upstairs he stopped for a brief moment to get into bed. Then he'd start again. Dad cried aloud while I cried silently.

We both cried ourselves to sleep.

What Dad didn't realize was how his injury and his attitude really impacted others.

Dad and I would frequently get into arguments over anything and he would say to me "What do you have to worry about? You don't have any problems! You're walking. You can move your legs. You carry on as though nothing has happened. I am the one who is stuck in a chair!"

I hated that.

"Yes I am not in a wheelchair like you are, but don't tell me my life isn't affected. I live with you and I care about you. Every day I now think about how you must feel. Do you think it's easy going around town having everyone ask me about you? I get so sick of it. I want to punch the lady at Tim Hortons. I can't even get a coffee without talking about you and your injury."

Soon Dad started to gamble more. He had won two thousand dollars at Casino Niagara a few months before his injury, and gambling was still on his mind. When he finally had a time when he didn't think he would soil himself, he would ask Mom to take him to the casino.

Friends joined him at first to hang out and support him, but as time went on Dad didn't slow down. His friends couldn't gamble as much as he did because they recognized that they still had bills to pay.

Dad felt like since he didn't get to enjoy his pension money through retirement that gambling would become his recreational activity instead. Dad gambled away his entire pension check every month until Mom finally convinced him to put a limit on it. Then he only lost half, because that was all that he could spend.

I tried to understand the best I could and cut my dad some slack. I know he appreciated my help fixing the house and doing what I could. His negative attitude about the whole thing just drained me. If I had a good day at school I would come home motivated to do some home-work. But the way he would talk just killed it. It was a painful environment to be in.

During this first year of his injury my sister Rebecca also had her own challenges. She didn't know how to deal with the tragedy at home and so she kept running off to stay at her boyfriend's house. I hated this and resented her for it.

When we needed the family to stick together and needed an extra hand with taking care of stuff, she wasn't around. I didn't have an escape, so my options were to either be stuck at home or ride my bike if I had the time. I forgive my sister completely now, but at the time it was a nightmare.

It just demonstrated again how much Dad's injury impacted every-one around him.

Life isn't fair. It never is, never has been, and never will be.

That is a good thing.

Because life isn't fair, each of us has an opportunity to set ourselves apart from everyone else. When you encounter some adversity in your life you have a choice about how you are going to handle it.

My dad chose to play the victim role. He chose to run away from the new challenges life presented him because he didn't think he deserved to get injured. He felt like he was robbed from retirement. The branch shouldn't have snapped. He acted as though he had the right to take out his anger and frustrations on Mom and everyone else because of his situation.

"You can't blame a tree.", I thought.

We all encounter unfair circumstances in our life. How can one person say getting cancer is fair? How about getting rear ended in a car crash? What if a stray bullet kills your child? Maybe someday you find you've been cheated on by your spouse. Did you deserve it? No. What happened to you may have been completely out of your control, but you certainly have control about how you are going to handle the situation.

I'm not going to tell you that it's easy to deal with because it isn't. I can tell you however that it's necessary.

I love the analogy of an archer using a bow and arrow. An arrow cannot be shot forward without first being pulled back. In order for it to propel forward a great distance with precision it needs resistance, to be pulled back. That arrow will never reach its target unless you hold it firmly and adjust it during that period of resistance. During resistance is when the arrow's aim is developed.

As a deer hunter my Dad should have understood that sometimes you have to hold an arrow back for a long period of time before the timing is right to release it. Your arm and fingers may be burning, but if you don't have patience and commit to the struggle you won't have the ability to gain clarity and narrow in on your target.

Life does this to us automatically.

I would not be where I am today had I not held on through the bad times. I had no idea when I was struggling in rehab that I would go on to play sledge hockey. Had I not kept my head afloat all these years I would not have a story to write this book. I had to hold on though and keep fighting, keep believing that what I was going through would pass and that someday it would all be worth it.

Nothing is going to change unless you change. Take responsibility for where you are today. If you are experiencing some trauma in your life consider that you may just have to hold on for a little while longer until the struggle is released.

Les Brown would say "Hard times have not come to stay, but they have come to pass."

If you feel you can't hold on during defeat, you decide to wallow in self-pity and resentment, when you are finally released you won't make it very far. You will just fall to the ground and be lifeless.

Don't be lifeless like my dad.

Hold on and be patient when you are faced with adversity. There is a reason you are going through your struggle and you have the strength to keep fighting. This period of time is necessary for you to find your target, and when you do discover it everything that you are fighting against will propel you forward.

Choose to stay in the fight.

CHAPTER 2

What's The Use Of College?

■ ■ ■

GOING TO COLLEGE WAS NEVER on my radar. I was having a great time in high school but the thought of it ending thrilled me. I couldn't wait to ditch the backpack and grab my riding gear.

Moving out was also not on my radar. Even if I wanted to I had no money and nowhere to go. Rent would cost money which I could use instead to gas up my dirt bike, so staying at home with Mom and Dad was fine with me. ... But it meant still playing by their rules.

Continuing my education after high school was one of the rules. I didn't want to go, so I put up a fight that first year. Dad and I got in some heated arguments about it.

"I don't want to go! I don't know what I would even take, so why are you making me go?"

"You have to go. Figure it out. If you don't go now you never will, and we have saved up so you can. This is what you're supposed to do."

Finally, reluctantly, I caved. "Fine, but it's just going to be a waste of your money."

Mom just held neutral on the whole situation.

In high school, I had done a six week co-op at Grimsby Electric. I got to thinking I would pursue that field, and ended up taking Electrical Engineering Technology at Niagara College. When I got into the class though, I ended up playing with circuit boards and doing a whole lot of complicated math, I was definitely not excited about any of it.

I soon formed a plan to escape college. To prove to my parents how badly I didn't want to be there and how wrong the decision was to force me to go, I started blowing through their money. I spent it anywhere I could.

I came home often saying, "I need money for a text book."

"I need money for another book too."

"My electronics kit is $300. I need money for that. ... Oh, and do you have money for gas?"

I needed my dad to feel the pain of what he was putting me through. I didn't want to waste his money but how else could I show him this was a bad idea?

Phase two of the plan was to fail classes. By the end of my first year I had barely passed my courses, averaging around 60%. I had even failed two of them with 40%. It was the first time I had ever failed a class. I hated that it would now be on my record permanently. I was proud of the fact that I had never failed and there I was staring at a report card that said 40% on it.

But it had to be done.

When the year was over I approached my dad again to ask him for some time away. He was reluctant but I said, "Look how badly I am doing and how much I hate going. Let me take some time off and I will go back. I promise."

Mom and Dad looked into the college fund program further and learned we could put the money on hold for up to two years, but then it had to be used or it's gone forever.

I took a year off and that's when I started bricklaying. The money was great and it was very tempting to stay, but I made a promise and would keep it.

At this point my sister was just getting into Brock University. She had way more book smarts than me and is incredible with numbers. Heading into her first year of accounting she already had $2000 in tuition grants thanks to her excellent grades and persuasive writing skills. Dad was definitely proud of her. She was killing it and hadn't even started.

I returned again to Niagara College, this time for a B.A. in Advertising & Marketing. I chose this because I thought it would be cool to learn to create a dirt bike magazine ad or possibly become a sales rep. I had a bit of design experience from high school as part of the yearbook committee where I had designed two pages on skateboarding and BMX biking. I figured that, as much as I could, I wanted to relate my education to dirt biking.

Finally I felt like I had a say as to why I was there. I met some great friends right away, and looked forward to going to school even if I wasn't thrilled about it. I still didn't know exactly where, when, or how this education was going to be used but one day it finally clicked.

I was in a web design program just learning basic fundamentals. We did HTML code, changing background colors and inserting photos when it came to doing our first project.

I asked my teacher if I could, for my project, build a website for me and my dirt biking friends. With his permission, I began building the Moto Freaks website, named after our riding group. Now I was hooked on college.

Years one and two of college turned out alright. It was in year two that Dad got hurt, so there was definitely some pain at that time, but school provided an escape for me.

Then one morning at 2:30am I got a call from my friend Mark. He was on his way home from the Red Hot Chili Pepper bar in St. Catharine's with a girl, and her car had broken down. Mark asked if I could come pick them up.

When I arrived Mark jumped into my car while the girl chatted with the tow truck driver. He smiled and said, "I think I'm going to move out to B.C.! Wanna come?"

Mark had been a big part of my life since Dad got hurt. We hung out on a regular basis, and I definitely felt like I would be losing a friend if I didn't join him.

"Well, I have to see if I can get a job and do my courses out there, but if I can, sure!"

I called my cousin Nicholas and he found me a placement at a moto-cross distribution warehouse working in the sales department. I did one bricklaying side job for my dad's friend for $800 to get some cash in my pocket, and two weeks later moved out west.

It was the first time I would live on my own. I was nervous, but things at home with Dad were becoming more negative by the day and I really wanted to get away.

Dad kept asking me why I wanted to leave. He didn't think there was any problem with staying at home and doing my courses in Ontario.

Mom however was very supportive of the idea. She saw what was going on between the two of us and said she could handle things at home. She encouraged me to go. It helped make the decision easier too, knowing that Rebecca was finally spending a bit more time at home again and the renovations had settled down.

Moving was one of the greatest things I could have done and it came at a great time. Building my website made me feel like I was getting closer to my goal of being a well-known rider. I was proud to show off that website to my friends. And now I was headed to one of the most beautiful places in Canada to go ride. I couldn't wait to see what the British Columbia mountains looked like.

When I was in college I had no idea where the skills I learned would take me. I think students often just do something because they have to. I sure did. Even if the courses seem interesting, it can feel pointless at the time because it's not something you see affecting the rest of your life.

I realize now how much college has helped me. I have built and designed four of my own websites. The first one promoted me as a bike rider and my last three marketed me as an athlete and public speaker.

With Photoshop I've been able to create documents for my business. I made event posters and designed my own business cards. Knowing how to navigate around a computer well allows me to solve more problems on my own instead of paying for help all the time.

Improving my English and getting better at writing has been very beneficial too. It's impacted my speaking career, blog, and the writing of this book.

The more things you can learn, the farther ahead you will be. You don't need to know it all, but it doesn't hurt to have an understanding in different areas of work. This gives you options.

As I drive down the city streets of Toronto I'll pass a group of skateboarders on the sidewalk. They'll have cameras out, capturing as much footage as they can. I'll watch them and wonder, "Do they have any idea how far these moments and experiences will take them?"

When I someday (hopefully) have kids, I don't plan to force them to go to college or university. College proved useful to me, and I will certainly encourage them to go, but as long as they have the drive to keep making something of their life then that's what I want to be supportive of, whether it involves college or not.

CHAPTER 3

Believing in Yourself

■ ■ ■

MOVING TO BRITISH COLUMBIA HAPPENED so fast. Mark ended up bailing on me last minute, but cousin Nicholas was willing to put me up so I went ahead anyway. During the drive there was some of the most beautiful scenery I've ever seen.

I remember gazing through the truck window at the immense beauty of mountains and valleys thinking, "This is cool. This is worth the risk to experience life."

When I walked in to work that first day, I felt like I had it made. Not because I was in sales - I had no idea how to sell anything - but because I was surrounded by dirt bike parts. A warehouse full of parts surrounded me, and I got to stare at product every day. Metal and plastic can get me really excited.

I quickly got to work selling on the phone but encountered a lot of challenges. At the time there was a change-over in the computer program so I made a lot of errors putting in product numbers and needed help. Also, despite loving the product, I still had a lot to learn about it in order to sell it. I felt like I was starting to get the hang of it when I got called into the boss' office.

"I'm sorry Kevin but I'm going to have to let you go."

"What? Why!?" I was stunned.

"Well, I can't afford to pay you."

I thought, "Then why the hell did you give me a job?!" But I realized he was trying to say, as nicely as possible, "You're not that good and I don't want you anymore." I kept my mouth shut and said thank-you for the opportunity. A little piece of wisdom I had picked up over the years was to never burn bridges. Besides, I had a feeling this path might come back around someday.

Thankfully Nicholas had another job to hook me up with. He was a control officer at a saw mill and got me a job there starting at sixteen dollars an hour. This was awesome because it was more than the twelve dollars I had been getting.

Unfortunately, I wouldn't get course credit for my work at the mill, so I had to keep looking for a sales position. I went out handing resumes to local motorcycle and skateboard shops.

Finally I got a call from Andrew at a local motorcycle shop who wanted an interview with me. I couldn't believe that I would possibly get to work at a bike shop for school credit. Andrew and I hit it off right away and I was hired. I went back to twelve dollars an hour, but it didn't matter. I was in a bike shop.

While I was there I got into a scene that I hadn't quite expected. These boys liked to party a lot. After hours we would hang out and drink and I tried cocaine a couple times. At the time I enjoyed it. To me it was a part of growing up that I needed to do. I felt like it was necessary to do as much bad shit as I wanted to while I was young so that when I got older I wouldn't feel like I missed out on anything. That's not to say try everything and don't worry about it. I am just lucky that recreational drugs never quite captured my attention.

Riding continued to be my guiding compass because if I was too messed up from partying, I couldn't ride.

During that time I also left Nicholas's and moved into a house with five other guys. It was fun for a while, but I was paying $800 a month for a tiny basement room, which only left me with a couple hundred dollars after my other expenses were paid.

I spoke to Andrew and he told me about this guy Lucas who sometimes came in. He was looking for a roommate and Andrew thought we'd be a good fit. He was right. When Lucas showed up one day, we chatted and hit it off right away, so we decided to go for it.

Lucas was older and rode Freestyle Motocross as well. He started to take me under his wing by introducing me to other riders, teaching me new tricks, and looking out for me when we were out partying in some of those new scenes. Good thing he did...

Some of his best friends had a good reputation for being wild and when we partied with them it got really messy. One night while I was smashed I got into a game of "Rock, Paper, Bottle" with a guy named Stones. The loser had to let the other guy break a beer bottle over their head. I lost, and Stones didn't aim right. Somehow the bottle didn't split, but my head did. Blood poured down the back of my neck.

Lucas took me to the hospital. While I was getting stitches he said, "You don't have to do that stuff. You can just walk away."

I loved having Lucas around because he treated me like his younger brother. He picked on me too, but he was always a solid guy, looking out for me while I struggled with all the shit in my life at that time.

I had become a bit disconnected from Dad, but whenever we got on the phone to touch base we would still argue. One day I got off the phone and was so mad I nearly started to scream. Lucas calmed me down and suggested we go to the skate park to let off some steam.

As we drove over there, Lucas told me his dad had committed suicide when he was younger. He never got to say goodbye and it was something that still haunted him. That was a real bonding moment for me. We both wished for better relationships with our dads.

The other defining moment with Lucas happened as we hung out with other riders who had their bike fenders cut shorter for freestyle riding. I had just gotten this brand new bike. It was the first and only one I'd ever bought new, I didn't want to cut it up even though that's what I wanted. I debated and debated it whether I should take a hack saw to it and make it into a different bike.

When I finally did it my life changed.

As I stepped back and looked at the newly shaped bike, I realized I hadn't just changed my bike, I had changed me. I was now a freestyle motocross rider. Until that point I was just a guy who rode trails and jumped, doing a few tricks when he could. But this was the commitment. Back then when you looked at a bike with grab holes in the side and cut fenders, you know that guy rides FMX. That day I became an FMX rider.

Doing drugs and partying hard while I was out in BC could have landed me in a pretty bad spot. It's so easy to get caught up in the wrong scene. I'm blessed that I had a solid friend in Lucas to remind me that you don't have to do what everyone else does just to fit in. Being yourself is cool enough. I loved being sober enough to ride. Riding was always my saving grace.

Just like in high school and all my jobs, everything revolved around my dirt bike. When I had to choose between partying and doing drugs or going riding, anytime I started to drift too far away from being able to ride, riding pulled me back. Time after time riding was my saving grace.

The whole fender cutting experience made me think a lot about what I was going to do when I returned home and finished school. I kept thinking about how my dad got the short end of the stick in life. Dad waited his whole life to live and now just one year from retirement he got robbed.

I didn't want to wait to live. I wanted to go in on my dream of being a professional FMX rider. I figured that if I could possibly die someday soon, I wanted to die knowing that I took the risks I wanted to. I didn't want to be in my dad's shoes thinking I should have lived sooner in life. I didn't want to miss my chance.

I talked with Lucas a lot about this before I left. As I was saying goodbye to Lucas that December some of his final words to me were "If you want to go for it man, I believe in you. You can do it." And that was it. If Dad didn't believe in me, at least Lucas did.

Sometimes we need others to believe in us until we believe in ourselves.

I left B.C. driving home to the song "Mission from God" by The Offspring singing the lyrics,

Yeah, I'm on a mission from God
It sounds kinda crazy but I like it a lot
I'm an answer to the man above
It's me he's been speaking of
Yeah, I'm just a fortunate son
Everybody wants to be the chosen one
I'm on a mission
I'm on a mission from God

I had my mind set on going in 100% to make this dream a reality. I felt it was my calling.

Sometimes when you don't believe fully in yourself, it takes someone else believing in you until you have the strength to believe in yourself. Thank you Lucas, you were that person for me.

CHAPTER 4

Living Obsessively

■ ■ ■

MOVING BACK HOME WENT PRETTY smoothly. The flat fields and straight open roads of the prairies aren't too exciting from inside a car, but it became more interesting as I thought about riding. Flat fields meant I could practice my wheelies or maybe jump the road from ditch to ditch. Riding breeds a creative mind, and it's fun to imagine something out of nothing. I didn't just love riding, I was obsessed by it.

When I arrived home it was the same as when I'd left. Dad's level of excitement was mediocre at best. Mom was still plugging away at work and Rebecca was going to school. It was a little calmer now that Dad had settled into a bit of a daily routine.

I returned to Niagara College and completed the rest of my marketing program. Dad attended graduation with me. That is one of my favorite memories and I will cherish it forever. I wasn't graduating for myself so much as I was graduating for him. I think Dad wanted it more than I did and I was happy to give that to him. Dad never completed more than high school, but back in his days that wasn't expected, or necessary. I was happy to make him proud.

While I was finishing up that semester I was dating a girl named Alice. She started to fall pretty hard for me and began talking about going camping together, visiting her family, and generally doing the whole relationship thing. I wasn't having any of that. I had plans every single weekend to go riding. Even if it was raining, I still wanted to be up north in Orangeville with my riding buddies.

One day we were leaving class and she asked me to come over to her place and hang out. I said that I didn't want to. I wanted to go home and chill, maybe work on my dirt bike. She kept pressing me to come, and wouldn't take no for an answer. I got angry.

"FINE! You drive and I'll follow you." Little did she know I had a plan.

I followed her out of the parking lot of Niagara College onto the Queen Elizabeth Highway heading east towards Toronto. We were crossing the Skyway bridge in St. Catharines, and her exit was coming up at the bottom. Instead of cutting off the highway with her I let her exit first, and then I just kept on going home. You can bet there was a call waiting for me when I arrived.

"What the hell was that!?" Alice yelled.

"I told you I didn't want to hang out. You wouldn't stop bugging me."

"You're an asshole, Kevin."

That's how I was back then. I didn't let anything get in my way of achieving my dream.

We broke up shortly after that.

After graduation, one of the guys I rode FMX with the most in Ontario, Tim, encouraged me to move up to Orangeville and ride with him full time. Tim helped hook me up with a masonry job, and offered that I could move in with him until I found a place. I agreed and moved in. I threw my bed in the corner of his basement where he stayed. It was great - we both got to sleep beside our bikes.

Howard Ranch was the home of Tim's friend, Steve Howard, who had a sick track out back in his field. It was the kind of track that every rider dreams of. We even had a bulldozer to make our own jumps.

Howard Ranch became my second home that summer and there was no other place in the world I would rather have been. Another of Tim's friends was Casey and he came out often to film. He captured so much of my riding life that year on camera. After a day of riding, we would always rush back home to watch the videos he'd taken.

Groups of friends would show up just to sit and watch me and Tim ride for hours on end as we learned new tricks. Coolers of beer were packed with gear bags. Punk rock, hip-hop, and heavy metal would always blast on the stereo. Just the process of getting geared up in the back of the pickup truck before we rode was one of my favorite things.

Just like Lucas, Tim also played a big role in helping me become a better rider. He would help me break down a trick to learn it step by step. We would discuss body positioning, timing foot movement when leaving the ramp, and how to work with the gyroscopic movement of the bike. We competed to see who was the best, but always while fully supportive of each other and helping each other improve.

To give you an idea of how complicated a stunt can be, here is a list of steps to learning the Superman Seat Grab:

First, get comfortable hitting the ramp and doing a No Footer.

Then start practicing a No Footer while taking one hand off the handlebar.

Do those two steps while simultaneously grabbing the grab hole under your seat with your free hand.

When you have a good sense of releasing your body and floating away from the bike, start to do these things while moving your hips back over the rear of the bike.

Work on getting your extension back as far as possible, beginning with your arms.

When you can do this with your arms fully extended, then work on straightening your legs in mid-air.

As you get comfortable hanging off the back of the bike, then it's time to work on your style and really throw your body as far away from the bike as possible.

Nowadays this is considered a very basic trick, but back in 2006 it had its place as a decent move to have in your bag of tricks. It's also fundamental to several of today's top FMX tricks that revolve around hanging off the back of the bike. Today you must also be able to do these things upside down.

We were so obsessed with riding that we would often pass out watching the videos of us riding in slow motion. We would study the video together and learn key moments where we could start a trick faster and adjust our body positioning to get full extension.

Whenever I wasn't passing out from work or studying videos, I would play MX Unleashed on Playstation 2 and get lost in video game life. Like dreamers we would have style contests over jumps and try to beat each other's times racing. If one of us flipped on the game by ourselves and saw the other had just knocked our name off the top of the leaderboard, we would race until we beat it.

Tim didn't work, so he had more time to race. I hated his video game skills. He owned a lot of podiums.

Video games may sound like a joke, but they actually help your mind focus a lot. Visualization is huge in any sport, and the more time you spend imagining yourself crossing the finish line first or scoring that winning goal, the greater chance you will have being prepared for the moment it actually happens.

That summer I learned the importance of surrounding yourself with people who are not only like-minded, but also better than you. Riding with Tim advanced my skill level much quicker than if I would have tried to learn everything on my own. Also, committing myself to riding on a regular basis and studying the sport in as many ways possible elevated my confidence. As time went on I got more comfortable, and then it didn't scare me as much to push the boundaries.

It's one thing to say you want to be the best but it's another thing to do whatever it takes to get there. I wasn't super confident about moving away from my parents' house for the second time. However, I felt if I didn't take some risk to go after what I wanted there was no way I was going to achieve my goal.

You have to be willing to take some risks or you will forever be trapped by your fears.

Be willing to challenge yourself because when you do, you grow. I didn't see it coming at the time but moving up to Orangeville was just another step in the bigger picture of this insane life I was only beginning to live.

CHAPTER 5

When Quitting Is A Good Idea

■ ■ ■

AS THE SUMMER OF 2005 was winding down my new masonry job continued to move ahead full force. Harry, my boss, was very good at finding work year round so I routinely put in forty and fifty hour work weeks.

This was definitely great for the paycheck but it took away all my riding time. Plus I was getting my ass kicked. Those longer hours contributed to fatigue. So whenever I was finished work it was either too late to ride or I was simply exhausted and needed to get some sleep and recover for the next day's work.

My plan to move up north to ride full time hadn't gone how I imagined it.

On top of this, Tim was getting in tons of riding time since he was unemployed. Just when I'd felt like I had caught up to him in skill level, he started to pull ahead again.

Thankfully, what little time we did have to hang out still revolved around talking about bikes. The Moto Freaks name continued to have a nice ring to it and we really wanted to put on some shows. I was excited to find a way.

We talked about how things could be done better in Ontario. The guy who was predominantly getting jump shows was Franks FMX, and we felt his events were poorly run. Frank had made a big impact on the sport in Canada years earlier when he was one of the first to jump freestyle. He also pioneered the idea in Canada of having a mobile landing ramp. Over the years though, his skill level never progressed and shows stayed the same. Tim and I definitely felt like we could do better. We just needed the ramps.

Using my skills from college, I drafted a business plan for Moto Freaks FMX shows. I came up with a S.W.O.T. analysis (strengths, weaknesses, opportunities, and threats) to look at what else Ontario had to offer. I came up with a budget, started sourcing suppliers, and looked at getting t-shirts printed.

I didn't care that Tim was unemployed or smoked a ton of weed, I just wanted a business partner who was as passionate about what we were doing as I was. Tim had updated the Moto Freaks website a few times so that was a nice contribution. Tim always hyped a lot of interest, but when it came down to doing the work though, I ended up doing the heavy lifting.

I kept asking Tim to make a few phone calls while I was at work to find some information on getting ramps built. Day after day though I would come home to see him sitting at his computer playing video games. I began to feel a lot of frustration and was definitely starting to question whether working with him was such a good idea.

Meanwhile back on the job site, Harry was also starting to get on my nerves. Harry was huge. Not fat, but tall. He was probably 6'5 and looked mean as hell. I don't think Harry had the best upbringing because he was always miserable and talked shit about other people who didn't have things as good as he did.

He had a beautifully large home in Hockley Valley which he built himself. He ran his own company, and worked extremely hard and extremely fast. There was a certain pace you had to keep up to, because if you couldn't follow Harry you would either get yelled at or you would be gone.

One kid in particular took shit from day one. His name was Jeremy and you could tell right away he had no confidence in himself. Harry tore strips off Jeremy's back every day.

"Jeremy, you piece of shit! What's the matter with you? Can't keep up? Maybe if your mom hadn't had sex with her brother you would have come out a little smarter! Get your ass over here!"

"Don't you feel lucky? I'm paying you twenty bucks an hour, giving you a job. You could be back at the paper mill working for twelve."

Some days I thought Jeremy was going to go AWOL. Harry was so mean to him.

When it came to talking shit like that to me, I was prepared to dish it back. Just like in the locker room, there's a bit of give and take on the job site. When it crosses the line however, you need to know when to go tell the other guy to fuck off.

Harry and I traded those blows a few times. After being pushed around in elementary school I wasn't about to let some prick like that talk to me. Even if he was my boss. The stuff Harry said was straight up brutal.

One day Harry was upset that we didn't get some scaffolding moved over quickly enough from one site to the next. Harry started yelling.

"You pieces of shit are useless. I ought to fire you and get some real help!"

I barked right back. "Then fire me! Don't talk to me like that. I don't deserve that shit."

I was sick of hearing this. I knew I was a good worker and I wanted to see if he actually would do what he said.

Harry turned around to say something, but then changed his mind and kept walking away. He never fired me and rarely said anything to me after that.

As winter approached, work slowed down some and guys would usually be laid off. That year for some reason, Harry hired another employee which only gave him another excuse to yell at our crew.

On January 2nd, 2006 I finally had enough. It was the day after New Year's and we were freezing our asses off in the middle of winter. Harry was once again bellowing at us about his superiority.

"Do you jerks have any idea how lucky you are? I could be lazy like every other boss out there and send you home on pogey for half your wage. Instead, I keep you employed so you can put food on the table and feed your girlfriends."

That day when we got back to the shop I told the guys in my carpool to hold on a minute. I went to Harry's front door and said "You say you have too many employees, right?"

"Yeah."

"Well let me help you take care of that problem then. Put me on E.I. I quit."

"Alright" he said, and we shook on it.

That was the last time I was ever going to be talked to that way by him.

You have a limited amount of time on earth. Jobs change. Relationships come and go. You have to make your time here count, and I was learning that there is no way I wanted to accept wasting my life away working a job for some employer who didn't appreciate the hard work I was putting in. I want to die knowing that I lived my life on my terms, and have no regrets about the choices I made.

The old guys on the job site influenced my decision as well. I had some great guys to work with. It was only Harry that was the problem. I loved shooting the shit with them. We're men and that's what we do.

Sometimes the older guys would say things like "When I was your age I could have been a pro football player" or "When I was your age I was going to travel the world".

"When I was your age..."

"What happened!?" I would ask.

"Well, I got a girlfriend."

"I was too busy partying."

"Weed got the best of me."

There was no way I wanted to be that old saying "I wish I would have, I could have, I should have."

If I wanted to go all in being a professional FMX rider, I needed to go for it. Some things in life only have a small window of opportunity to become a reality and this was one of them. At the age of 23 I figured I would have another five to seven years before I would have to quit, if everything went well.

I got together with my mom and grandmother as well to hear what they had to say. I knew I couldn't ask my dad. It was obvious he would say no. I wanted to know that I had some support at least from someone in my family as there was a good chance I'd be needing their help for this someday.

Hearing my mom say, "I support you" meant a lot and that was the last piece of affirmation I needed to quit my job and go for my dream. Don't get me wrong, I had backup plans. I didn't just quit impulsively. But I also know that to succeed you can't have only one foot in the water.

If I hadn't walked away from that job then I think I would still be a bricklayer. I would be working along the same type of guys talking the same type of shit and always regretting not taking the chance.

As a result of my choice, I live in physical discomfort every day and have gone through some emotional battles, but I am always thankful that I took the risk. I truly feel like I could die happy. I've lived my life on my terms and make the most of every day I have on this planet.

From my experience it's been clear that you have to commit to yourself that you are willing to face whatever hurdles and obstacles come your way.

It takes an extreme amount of courage because you don't always know what the path will look like or where it may lead. Becoming an entrepreneur is a lot like taking a vacation that goes wrong on a regular basis. You find ways to make it enjoyable because if you know that if you quit and go back to "regular life" that at some level you know you won't be reaching your full potential.

Successful people don't always make the right decisions. They choose, however, to make their decisions right.

I never thought on January 2nd, 2006 when I walked off the job site that day that I would still be on this vacation 10 years later. It sure has been crazy, and as you're about to learn this was just the tip of the iceberg.

CHAPTER 6

When Quitting Is Not An Option

■ ■ ■

RIGHT AROUND THE TIME I quit my job, two other major events happened.

First was I was moving out of Tim's basement. It was only supposed to be temporary and I wanted to keep to my word on that. Tim's mom was starting to get a little weird so I made moving a priority. She was a painter, and I think she sniffed a few too many paint brushes in her time. Some days she would be really happy I was there and other days she would ask how soon I'd be moving out.

I found a nice place in Hockley Valley, just ten minutes away from the ranch. After I had moved most all the stuff myself, Tim joined me for a ride over there to see the new place.

The second event was that our relationship was about to change. Since Tim had been doing next to nothing the entire time I was living with him, I got to see what kind of a business partner he would be. I'd put in over forty hours a week and come home to see him stoned at the computer playing video games. It gave me zero confidence that things would work out.

It was on my mind for a while to do the business on my own, and it was time to break the news to him.

"So listen" I said "I have a question for you. We have been working on trying to do this Moto Freaks business plan for a while and I think there's a lot more to do. If we go further with this what are you expecting to get out of the deal if we sell stuff and get shows?"

"Well I would want half" he said.

Yeah right.

"Well, since we've been working on this you haven't been putting in half the work and I don't think I'm ready to go in to business with you if it's like that. What do you think about if I were to start the company under my own name and I'll just hire you out to do jump shows? I've already come up with a name, Underground FMX Productions."

"I guess, man. Sure." Tim didn't seem to care.

I didn't enjoy feeling like I was stealing Tim's thunder. Moto Freaks was a sick name he came up with and I loved riding with the boys under that name. I knew that if I wanted to do this right though, that I had to do it on my own, so Underground FMX became the new Moto Freaks.

I started refining my business plan the next day. I changed a couple things around to say Underground FMX. I started a brand new website. I made posters and flyers. My initial ambition didn't exist without some hurdles right from the get go. I had a female roommate in that house, probably somewhere in her forties, and she was an absolute nightmare to live with. We only had dial up internet at that time so if I was using the internet, she couldn't use the phone.

Not that she didn't have options. She did have a cell phone and was never home during the day anyway. I didn't have a phone jack in my room so I ran a long cord through the hallway. This girl would disconnect my cord while I was working causing me to lose my internet connection always screwing up my work. One day she even locked me out of the room with the phone jack! I would break into her room with a butterknife when she wasn't home and then use her phone jack. Ridiculous stuff, just to have internet.

When I finally got the business plan together I headed to the bank for a loan. Thankfully, since my parents had instilled good habits in me of always paying my bills on time, I had some killer credit. I was quickly approved for $20,000 without a co-signature. I was in business.

The next task was to figure out where I would get ramps built. I needed a portable take-off and landing ramp in order to put on these shows, and there were fewer than five people in North America that I knew of who had one.

I contacted a guy down in Indiana, Pennsylvania whose business Hardcore FMX built ramps. Let's call him Dick. I don't remember Dick having a website, but I'd seen his ramps in photos and videos with big name FMX riders jumping off them. It seemed legit.

After speaking to Dick on the phone, he said he could give me everything I needed and all within my budget. Dick said he had a landing ramp currently being built in his shop and I could check it out first hand. I also asked how much of a deposit he would need.

"$10,000 on a $15,000 project." he said.

"I'll bring $5,000 down."

I hopped on a plane to go down to Indiana and see him in person. Dick picked me up at the airport, and on the drive to his house, we talked bikes. His shop looked good and the ramp that was in production was just what I was looking for. I followed him into his office and gave him the $5,000 money order.

I should have never handed him that cash. Things seemed too perfect. The invoice was only half a page for a $15,000 piece of one-off equipment. Dick had been short and rude on phone calls with other people while I was there too, but I just ignored the warning signs. I wanted the ramps so bad.

We hopped back in his truck and he drove me to my overnight hotel. Conversation was slower now. There seemed to be a lot less interest in chatting, and my gut was starting to sink. When I got to the hotel we shook hands, said thank you, and goodbye. The moment I stepped out of his truck and looked at his face while I shut the door I knew I was screwed.

Dick kept things nice enough for long enough to get the other half of the deposit. I sent it to him within a few days despite my gut telling me no. Dick already had $5,000 of my money. He was not going to give it back anyway, so I thought I'd keep ignoring the warning signs and just see what happens.

I didn't tell anyone how I was feeling. What a horrible mistake.

Dick never answered my calls after that. He returned them days later, or he would email me a reply. Getting him on the phone was impossible.

On top of all that, he wanted me to pay for additional ramp features that we had already agreed were included in the price. I had no argument though, because my invoice sucked and was not detailed. Now I KNEW I was getting screwed and I couldn't even do anything about it.

On top of all this, riding was soon becoming a job and no longer a hobby. I used to love riding for so many reasons. I'd get to hang out with my friends. I would spend the day relaxing at the track. We'd pushed each other to learn new tricks for fun. But now I felt like I had to push to even compete. If I was going to put on shows in Ontario I had to be one of the best riders. Riders gauge each other by their bag of tricks and I needed to keep adding to mine.

I didn't see this coming.

I put myself in some pretty uncomfortable positions learning new tricks that spring of 2006. You're supposed to be relaxed and focused while learning. Instead I would ride when exhausted from working overtime laying bricks during the week. I was forcing myself to do something I didn't want to, while risking my life on jumps that could kill me.

This was a recipe for disaster.

Meanwhile, Tim started to really distance himself from me. He would ride throughout the week while I was at work and then say he was too tired to ride with me on the weekend. He still didn't have a job so he could have easily waited for the weekend. Since he chose not to, I ended up riding alone.

I didn't know what was going to happen, or if this riding thing was ever going to work out, but I had to keep on going.

I still struggle at times with success not happening fast enough. I look back on the experience with Dick and learn from it, hoping I never jump into something so quickly again.

Don't give up. See it through to the end. This is the attitude I've lived by and still do. I had no idea if pursuing sledge hockey would ever work out. I took on being a landlord with no experience at all. I feel like I've flopped at speaking sometimes, but I keep on going.

In the words of Eric Thomas "You have to be persistent with the action, and patient with the outcome."

That's what I live by. Though, I have to consistently remind myself to be patient.

CHAPTER 7

When You Start Hating What You Love

■ ■ ■

I KEPT PRESSING ON.

Even if Dick was going to try and screw me over with the ramps, I would keep my commitment and move forward in other areas of the business. It was a huge gamble to start booking shows without the ramps in my drive-way, but I kept faith that things would eventually work themselves out.

Two major summer events at the time were Wakestock and Jump Fest. These competing events each put on a show involving wakeboard-ing, skateboarding, FMX, and a ton of music artists. The crowds there were big, so I really wanted to get paid to jump there someday.

For smaller events, riders jump at local fairs. Fairs offer less pay but there are more of them, some offering a show or two per month. I found out the Ontario Association of Agricultural Societies puts on a trade show each spring in Toronto for the fairs to pick out their entertain-ment, so I booked a booth there.

The trade show went well and was a ton of fun. I brought my entire desktop computer, monitor, and cables to the event so I could play my demo video. I had my inquiry forms, business cards, and posters. I felt like this was what I had dreamed of - doing things legit.

Lots of people showed interest at the time but only a few ended up calling. One guy I spoke with was in charge of the show at the Lindsay fairgrounds. His name was Peter.

He and I had good talk but Peter ended up hiring another FMX rider, Matt. That was no big deal. Then I bumped into Peter about six weeks later at another event. He pulled me aside to chat, and said he hadn't heard back from Matt in over six weeks. He had no idea if Matt would even show up to the fair or not.

"Would you be willing to come ride for me?" Peter asked.

"Yes of course!" This was the chance for my first FMX show ever!

I offered that I could rally two other riders to join me; Tim and my friend Troy. My ramps weren't going to arrive in time but Troy said he could bring his take-off ramp and Peter said he would build us a dirt landing. We would get paid $1000 each to jump four shows over the course of two days.

Peter and I shook on it and I emailed him a contract later that night.

I called Tim and told him I had landed our first gig. The date was set for Canada Day weekend at the Lindsay fairgrounds. I could hardly believe we were getting a grand each.

"That's sick man. ...I want $1500 though." Tim sighed into the phone.

"Dude, it's our first show. This is what he offered and you need to take it."

"Well are we getting a hotel room comp'd too?"

"Yes."

"Food?"

"I don't know." Tim's demands were starting to get on my nerves.

"Well I need food comp'd too."

"Ok man! We'll figure it out. I'll buy you your food if I have to."

I didn't know why Tim was acting this way. I was just happy to get the gig. Up until this point we were just backyard riders with a cool name.

We arrived at the Lindsay fairgrounds on Friday morning. To our surprise, a truck and ramp were parked, ready and waiting. Inside, the driver slept soundly. After six weeks of not responding to any calls, Matt had shown up after all.

We introduced ourselves and started to set up. Instead of using Troy's ramp we used Matt's. I was resentful that Matt was there since I thought the show was ours, but as long as we were all still getting to ride

I was good with things. Another rider I didn't know showed up, Stu. He was pretty good.

Tim was quick to abandon me, eager to buddy up with Matt. I had Underground FMX shirts printed and Tim refused to put one on at first. Matt did (I think only because he had no clean clothes) and then Tim eventually did too.

The weekend show went awesome and I soon realized I was finally accomplishing my childhood dreams.

1. I got paid to ride my dirt bike.
2. I jumped in front of a crowd.
3. I signed autographs for little kids.
4. I was in a magazine ad through one of my sponsors.

Everything I had ever dreamed of was coming together and I felt like my hard work was starting to pay off. Peter thanked me for helping set everything up and ensure his event went smoothly. I was just happy to see one person not feel like they were getting screwed out of their show. Had I not bumped into Peter in the weeks prior, he may have waited until the day of the show to find out if Matt arrived or he may have not at all.

On Monday I went right back to laying bricks. Tim and I didn't talk much that week. On Friday I called to see if he wanted to go riding. He never answered the call.

I went to the track on Saturday with my buddy Lube and figured I would get in some practice on my own. I was talking with Lube about the whole ordeal and decided to give Tim a call again. When he answered the phone it was very loud in the background.

"Tim, what's up man."

"Not much dude. Just chillin. You?"

"I'm at the track. I wanted to see if you'd come ride and get some practice in?"

"Ah, I can't man. I'm at the Molson Indy in Toronto with Matt."

"You're what!?"

Apparently Tim and Matt had hit it off at the Lindsay Fairgrounds and Matt invited Tim to ride at the Molson Indy.

"How much are you getting paid for that?"

"$500 bucks."

You were demanding $1500 just a week ago at a local fair and now you're willing to sell yourself short at $500 in front of the entire city of Toronto!? What are you doing!?

I was gutted. This guy was supposed to be my best friend and now he's going behind my back to ride for less money than I got him, and didn't even tell me about it.

I hung up the phone.

The following weekend Jump Fest was coming up. I had been in negotiations with the promoter about bringing my ramps and doing a show. But, since my ramps were nowhere to be found, he ended up going with Franks FMX.

I was pissed to see Frank get another big show and the promoter kept asking if I would come ride for free on Frank's ramps. The last thing I wanted to do was help any of those guys.

Still, I hummed and hawed about it the whole week and then on the last night before the event I decided to go. I had this vision in my mind that I would show up and ride really well showing everyone in attendance that I was the best rider. I would go home with my chest puffed out and then continue working on getting my ramps so I would never have to jump someone else's again.

When I started my Underground FMX business I had no idea things would have been this challenging. I expected things to go smoothly. The phone was supposed to be ringing off the hook. I was sure that everyone would see what I was trying to do and come running to me for help. People were to pay what I asked for in show pricing, and my ramps sure as hell would have shown up on time. I also expected Tim and I would stay best friends and continue to ride as much as we could.

I was doing good things. Why was all of this happening to me?

Maybe the bigger question was how can so many people operate in this world without integrity?

Riding at Jump Fest ended up being a bad idea. I was going there entirely out of spite and for no good purpose at all. It didn't matter how loud my gut was screaming at me to stay home. I felt like I had something to prove and that I needed to show the world what I was made of.

I was so mad at Tim that I didn't even want to look at him. Tim's going to the Molson Indy proved his carelessness and selfishness. Matt was just another Frank and those were guys that I didn't want to associate myself with.

The fact that Dick was still avoiding all my calls and delaying the ramp building process made me wonder if summer would end before anything showed up. Bricklaying continued to pay the bills, but I was living pay check to pay check.

What was I to do?

Riding was something I started because I loved it, and now not only was it a job, it was becoming something I hated. Everything that I had worked so hard to achieve, I now wanted to avoid. It would have been much easier to cancel the ramp order and just go back to riding Howard Ranch as a backyard guy. I was in too deep.

Different risks carry different costs. It may be losing money. It may require risking a relationship. In the sport of Freestyle Motocross, you risk your life. You don't have an option to not be in a good mindset or on top of your game when you jump 90-foot gaps.

As I was about to find out, things were about to get a lot worse.

CHAPTER 8

The Accident

■ ■ ■

I REMEMBER EVERYTHING ABOUT THAT morning vividly.

When I woke up I didn't like the feeling in my gut. I was mad that I was going to Jump Fest. I didn't want to jump for free and I sure as hell didn't want to see Frank.

I was also pissed at Dick for the ramps not having been built yet. If they had been built and had arrived on time I would be staying home to practice instead. I would much rather have been doing that.

And, because I didn't have Tim coming to jump with me, I also felt alone. I wished things were different. I wanted him to come, but he wasn't interested.

I had a bowl of cereal for breakfast and went out to the garage to load up my bike. The neighborhood was quiet and peaceful. Loading the bike in the stillness of early morning is so serene. I have always enjoyed that process and to me it's part of the love of riding.

Casey pulled up as planned, eager to come film the show. We got on the road early. It was nearly a three hour drive from Orangeville to Haliburton, Ontario where Jump Fest was being held.

When we arrived we went over to the show area to check out the setup. Frank was there standing around with his riding buddies. I introduced myself.

"Hey. So you're the Rempel guy?" Frank said.

Neither of us was impressed to meet the other. He definitely knew who I was though, and that I was coming for him.

I noticed another guy hanging around. It was the additional rider, Stu, from the Lindsay fair. Stu was a good guy, and had come with his girlfriend. We decided to all go for lunch before our 2:00 practice.

Lunch was good, but it didn't matter because my stomach was still so sick. I didn't want to be there but I felt it was too late to back down on my commitment. I also didn't want to admit how nervous I was.

Around this time my phone rang and it was Tim. "Hey man, do you know if they have any spots still available to jump today?" I thought, "Are you kidding me?!"

"You're too late." I said, and hung up the phone.

By the time we finished lunch it was almost time to get ready for practice. We walked back to our pickup trucks parked alongside the show area and started getting ready.

To give you an idea of the setup, here's what it looked like.

In riders terms, we don't speak in MPH or of how many feet we were in the air. We speak of the distance of the gap and the gear our bike is in when we hit that jump. At this show there were two ramps set up. One was at a distance of 45 feet and one at 75 feet. Just from knowing the gap itself, I knew I would hit them in 2nd and 3rd gear, respectively.

The ramps themselves were like what I'd ordered from Matt. They were both steel take-off and landing ramps. Riders would always practice on dirt landings at home, but steel was the way to go for shows.

Normally one ramp would be set up centered and squared to the landing ramp. Since there were two, they were both angling in towards the landing instead of square. There also was no safety airbag. In addition, the wind was blowing. It wasn't blowing too strong to ride, but I never liked jumping in the wind and this added to my discomfort.

To make matters worse, Frank's 75 foot ramp had a brutal transition to it. The transition is the curvature of the ramp as you take off. Back in the Evel Knievel days ramps were just straight pieces of wood built up off the ground. Now, in the sport of FMX, different ramps were being experimented with to see what had the best transition for a rider to get a "pop" from the ramp. We could definitely ride this ramp, but it wasn't the greatest.

Everything was doable. I had jumped 90 foot gaps at Howard Ranch on a regular basis, but that was home.

All these factors continued to play in my head as I got dressed in my truck. Having Casey around helped me feel a little more comfortable, but he soon took off to film outside the riding area so he could get a better angle. The thought kept churning in my mind, "You shouldn't do this."

This was a recipe for disaster. You have to be focused to ride. Big gaps were my thing, but given all the distractions in my mind and my gut screaming at me, it was the worst decision to ride.

Stu got ready before me and started to warm up his bike. As he did, more spectators started to run over to the fence to watch. Seeing crowds form just from the sound of the bikes always excited me.

My nervousness grew.

Stu started going up and down alongside the ramps to clear the engine out and I then fired up my bike to do the same. I felt like everyone was watching us. Probably because everyone was.

Stu started to hit the ramp and jump the 75 foot gap. His first hit was so smooth. He had jumped Frank's ramp before and this was my first time ever. I kept warming up my bike hoping the nerves would go away.

Stu hit the ramp a couple more times and by now I felt like people weren't even watching Stu, I felt like they were watching me and wondering "What's taking this guy so long?"

The pressure I was putting on myself was way too much. I should have taken my time and done some speed checks with Stu but didn't. I decided to just go for it.

I lined up to hit the ramp. Two taps down on the shifter let me know I was for sure in first gear. One shift up with my boot put me in second. I accelerated towards the ramp.

As I sped on, I felt the bike sputter a bit. "Maybe it's just in my mind." I thought. I shifted into third gear. The ramp quickly rose in front of me and I took off.

"Oh no" I thought. I knew I wasn't ready for it.

The transition of the ramp had kicked the rear end of my bike higher than the front. The ramp transition had something to do with it, but the bigger issue was that I wasn't focused and relaxed to properly absorb the impact. As I left the tip of the take off ramp, I knew I had a decision to make.

If I stayed on the bike, there was a good chance I would clip or land on the safety deck of the ramp and head dive into the ground. If I jumped off the bike I could try to land on my feet and break my legs. The better case scenario was to save my neck, so I decided to jump off and break my legs.

Because we caught the whole crash on video, I could later see what had happened. As I pushed off the bike I jumped through the handle-bars. When I pushed off, I pushed too hard and my feet came up in the air and didn't provide me the cushion to break my fall. I landed - without the bike – right on my ass near the bottom of the landing. Probably another three to five feet and I would have landed on flat ground.

"UGH!"

I felt like I had been hit by a transport truck. It happened quickly but I didn't lose consciousness. I laid there on the ground and gasping for air, just like my dad had when he fell from the tree.

Paramedics ran over and were immediately over my head asking me questions like "Do you remember what happened? Do you know where you are?" Before I could answer any questions I just tried to get the air back into my lungs. Then, when I caught my breath a bit, I tried to move.

I was laying on my left side in the fetal position with my legs crossed. I could see my legs and tried to uncross them. I couldn't.

Then I put my hand on my leg to push it off. When I did, I couldn't feel it. That's when I looked up to the sky and said, "Oh fuck. I'm paralyzed."

The very next thought that ran through my head was, "Dad told you so."

It was very ironic. The scene was so much like my dad's injury. Today I often think a person could not write this script. It's unbelievable that both Dad and I were now paralyzed. The same questions were being asked over my head as I laid there that had been asked over his. We both had the air knocked out of our lungs, and we both now were paralyzed.

Casey pushed his way through the paramedics and threw his hand out to me.

"I got you buddy. I love you bro. Don't worry, everything is going to be ok."

"Thanks man." I said, taking his hand, "You better be filming this."

Riders *always* want their crash on film! If you're going to go down hard, you can at least make things worthwhile by having a video to relive the moment. It sounds a little psychotic, but that's what we were as riders. I was already thinking about making that comeback movie.

Little did I know that comeback wouldn't happen for quite some time.

As I laid there, I could feel my broken back with any slight movement. The best way to describe it is to compare it to having a large butcher knife stabbed directly into your spine. Any sudden movement was the knife being twisted.

It took some time but I finally got loaded onto a stretcher. The sky was all I could see until I got into the ambulance and then I started to drift in and out of memory. I remember feeling every bump in the ambulance ride over to the Haliburton hospital. I didn't know where I was headed at the time. All I knew was that I wouldn't be showing up to work on Monday and I wouldn't be riding my bike for some time.

Life was about to get really hard.

CHAPTER 9

The Hospital

■ ■ ■

THROUGHOUT THE WHOLE ORDEAL, CASEY was incredible. Not only did he call my mom immediately to let her know what happened, but he kept filming. Casey followed the ambulance to the hospital and captured some footage there until they told him to shut off the camera. In America, many riders have even captured the whole surgery on film. I wasn't so lucky.

After Haliburton, I was quickly air lifted down to Sunnybrook Hospital in Toronto. There was a large team of staff awaiting my arrival as I was in critical condition. I can still remember the excruciating pain as I was transferred back and forth between the stretcher and the tables for many scans before they could operate.

First I was transferred from the helicopter into the hospital. Then I was passed into a chamber for an MRI, then back to the stretcher. Then I went to another table for x-rays, then back to the stretcher, all without any pain medication.

I was screaming with pain.

At this point I don't remember anything else until I woke up in the Intensive Care Unit three days later. At that point I knew that I had broken my back and was groggy as hell. There was a bag beside me filled with morphine and I barely had enough strength to lift my eye lids let alone my arms. A catheter led to another bag beside me. I couldn't feel my legs and it was scary.

The good news is that I only have a few memories of ICU as I was mostly sleeping while I was there.

I remember Casey's parents were the first ones I saw there. It was purely coincidental, because I know my mom came immediately. I spoke with them a bit and then caught up with my mom next. She wasn't mad either, just incredibly supportive. She promised she would be there for me.

Thinking about it now, I can't imagine what my mom must have been thinking as she stood beside my bed knowing both her husband and son would be in wheelchairs, possibly for the rest of her life. She had to wonder what she signed up for.

You know what my mom would say? For better or for worse. Those were the vows she took when she married and she will live by them until the day she dies. That's how incredible my mom is.

Dad, on the other hand, chose not to come. I knew that he didn't want to see that familiar environment ever again.

As a nurse worked by the bed, she informed me that my surgeries weren't over. Only one had been done immediately to fix my broken back. I still needed one more surgery to fix my broken pelvis.

Basically here is how you can understand the fractures. In my back, I had what's called a fracture/dislocation of my T12 and L1 vertebrae. Your T12 vertebrae is what connects to your bottom rib, between your belly button and your chest.

My spinal cord had been pulled and pinched into a zig zag. My top vertebrae had shifted back causing pressure on the spinal cord and cutting off any nerve signals sent down to my feet. Surgery realigned the vertebrae, but because of the trauma, swelling, and pressure built up around the area, doctors were all left uncertain if anything would ever come back.

In my pelvis I had what's called an open book pelvis fracture. You can imagine what this means. My pelvis was split wide open right at the bottom, like a book. It's an incredibly thick bone to break and it hurt like hell.

Because of those injuries and a few fractured ribs I had a lot of internal bleeding. They couldn't operate all at once, so I went back in for the pelvis surgery and woke up again on day four in Sunnybrook's general ward.

When I woke up I heard a guy moaning and groaning beside me. I wasn't stoked about that but at least I could move around a little better now. I also couldn't complain about the window facing a brick wall, because I was happy to see some sunlight again.

I remember the first time my doctor came in. Like any typical doctor, he was in a rush. It helped that I had already been injured so many times before, so my expectations of him were pretty low. I didn't expect him to stay very long. He walked in and asked me how I was doing.

"I'm doing good, thanks." I jumped right to the point. "What's the prognosis here?"

"Well Kevin, you're now an incomplete paraplegic and will likely never walk again. If you do by chance ever happen to walk again you'll walk with braces on your legs up to your hips the rest of your life."

"Is that it?" I asked.

"Anything more, we don't know."

"Ok. Thanks."

I don't remember being upset. I didn't cry. That's just how it was. I didn't want him to give me any soft, sugary story about what the deal was. Just give it to me straight.

After he left I thought about my situation. I could be upset about it, but I had caused this myself. I had to take responsibility for my situation. There was no one to blame but me.

My chances felt like one in a million. Yes, recovery was a long shot. Everything was completely unknown at that time, but to me recovering was nothing more than a simple process. You get injured, have surgery, do therapy, and get better. That's all there was to it. I didn't see it any other way.

I tell people now that it definitely helped me to be naive about the situation. I actually called my bricklaying boss that week and told him what happened. I said that I had broken my back but I expected to be out of the hospital and walking again in 8 to 12 weeks.

"Can you hold my spot on the line for me?" I asked.

"Yeah…. let's chat again when you're ready to come back and see where things are."

The last thing I remember about those first few days in hospital is an old man randomly walking into my room to hand me a business card. Just like my doctor, he was also very quick. Almost like he wasn't supposed to be there.

This old man came in and quickly says "Hey, I just want to pass this onto you, in case you decide to call a lawyer. These guys are good."

"No thanks man. I don't need it. I don't plan to call any lawyer." I said. I was very much against calling a lawyer. I'd heard too many stories of other riders around North America suing motocross track owners for an injury they sustained on their property, forcing the track owner to go out of business. As much as I hated all that went down at Jump Fest, I didn't want to be that guy.

"Well, I'll leave it with you anyway in case you change your mind. I think it might be worth giving them a call to see if they can help."

"Ok, thanks man."

And he vanished.

To this day I still have no idea who he is. I don't know where he came from, why he picked my room, what his name was, or where he went after that. Later on, that moment proved to be one of the biggest godsends ever that could have happened. I would like to see that guy now.

The comeback story is what everybody loves. I knew my injury and believed recovery was possible. Just like Casey had kept filming, I was going to keep recovering.

Being naive definitely helped with the confidence, but I soon started to learn what life with an SCI (spinal cord injury) can be like.

Similar to what amputees get, they have phantom pain when they lose a leg, I was getting phantom pains in my bowels. I felt like I had to take a shit. I felt like I could push, but nothing would come out. I later learned it was nerve damage making me think something was there, when it actually wasn't.

l felt so uncomfortable that the nurses gave me a suppository to help stimulate things. A suppository is a little white bullet shaped piece of wax that is inserted in the butt, dissolves, and tickles the rectum, causing you to poop.

When that didn't work, they tried an enema. Enemas treat constipation by introducing fluid into the intestines through the rectum. The liquid softens impacted stool, while the enema nozzle loosens the rectum. That combination stimulates a large bowel movement.

I laid sideways on that bed for nearly ten minutes with a swimming pool of water going through my ass trying to take a shit. I was screaming at the nurse "It's almost there!" only to learn there was nothing there at all. This SCI was starting to not be so easy to get over.

After a few days some great friends show up. My buddy Rick came out of the blue and brought me a portable DVD player with nearly ten sport bike and dirt bike DVD's. I had a cell phone, but couldn't play videos or music from it. This was back when iPod's and iPhone's still weren't in existence. I was so pumped Rick brought me that stuff. It really helped keep me sane while time passed by.

Shortly after that, Casey showed up with a bunch of guys to cheer me up. Tim was there, as well as many of the guys I rode with at Howard Ranch. I remember trying to just forget about all the stuff that had happened with Tim. My entire life could have been different had he and I still been tight.

Maybe we would have been hanging out together and both said "Screw going to Jump Fest." I could have been hanging out at Howard Ranch riding with him, but instead I went to the show on my own and crashed. Still, I knew that even if I was pissed at him, I was responsible for my situation. I did this, not Tim.

The boys and I had a good visit and we chatted about how gnarly the crash was. It wasn't the most graceful way to go down, but I was proud to have done it doing something I loved. I always felt like if I were to go down and be injured, I want to be injured riding my bike rather than something like a car wreck or a bar fight.

The last thing I remember about my time in the hospital was dealing with that asshole Dick. My ramps still had to be dealt with and now this guy decided to call me.

"Hey man, I heard about your crash. How are you doing?"

Like you give a shit.

"I'm fine. What's going on."

"Just wanted to give you an update on things. Still working away. It's going to be another few weeks until your ramp is finished."

"Yeah well that doesn't really matter to me right now. I'm paralyzed in bed."

"Sorry to hear man. I hope you get better soon. I'll give you a shout when it's ready to come pick up."

Like I could come pick it up. As if I wanted to think about that right now. I swear that this guy haunted me the entire time about my injury. I just wanted him out of my life.

CHAPTER 10

One Toe At A Time

■ ■ ■

ONE THING THAT CAN MAKE any guy perk up is a hot nurse. My hospital stay at Sunnybrook hadn't warranted any major excitement, but when I got transferred over to Lyndhurst, Toronto Rehabilitation Institute's facility for spinal cord injury patients, I honestly felt like I may have just hit the jackpot.

Her name was Lisa. She had blonde hair and a sexy body. And to top it all off, she was cool.

It was only a couple of days into the new facility when I was being pushed to start moving around. I didn't think I was ready, but when someone pushes you, you start to realize you're actually stronger than you think you are.

I began by just gathering my marbles while sitting up on the edge of the bed. After lying down for two weeks straight I had trouble with sitting. All the blood would rush to my head and I would feel like passing out. Once we got that dialed down, my task was just learning to rock side to side and discover what pain tolerance I had for moving around.

Eventually I had to graduate from the bedside for bowel movements to the actual toilet, and this meant pushing the limits even more. Because my body still wasn't strong enough to get there myself, we had to use some tools. In addition to a suppository, a hoist and sling were needed to transfer me from the bed to the commode chair.

The suppository took some time to brew. They average five to ten minutes before you need to be over the toilet seat, so after five minutes I would get loaded up in the sling. Mid transfer, as I hung in the sky like a baby being carried by a stork, my butt started to leak from the magic bullet in my ass. Body fluid leaked all over the floor, right in front of Lisa. All my manliness washed away faster than they can call for "Cleanup by Rempel's bedside."

Thank God she didn't make me feel embarrassed. She actually laughed, and made a joke about it.

"Ahh, don't worry about that. You'll get used to it. I certainly have."

"Thanks Lisa." I thought.

It's easy to laugh about that stuff now but when you're going through it, you feel like you've just been stripped of all your dignity.

The next challenge I had was to try to stand, even before I could feel or move my legs.

My therapist, James, had me wheel my chair over to him. He then locked his feet in front of mine. I then shuffled to the edge of my wheelchair seat and put my knees to his knees. James instructed me to put my hands on top of his shoulders and pull myself up as he grabbed my bum and pulled my hips towards him. The idea was to have my body act like a scissor lift and open itself up from the seated position. I have never felt so overwhelmed, and it was at this moment when I broke.

As I began to stand with his help, I started shaking from being so stiff and so weak and began to bawl my eyes out.

"I can't do this James! I don't want to do this! I can't!" And I sat down. It was too much for me that day, and I wheeled back to my room to cry.

I thought "How am I ever going to get better?" Reality was punching me in the gut and I wondered if this was even possible.

I kept going back to physiotherapy asking that same question every day.

"You just have to try." James said. "Try to wiggle your toe. Every day spend some time and work on it. You have to wake up the nerves because they are in shock from all the trauma."

"Ok" I thought, and decided to take that on seriously.

When I looked around Lyndhurst I realized I wasn't the only one who was feeling that way. There were many other people who had just arrived and were uncertain about their future. Many sustained injuries from being pushed off a balcony, a roof, or even a tailgate. Others accidents included shallow diving, rolling a four-wheeler down a hill, or crashing while water skiing.

Regardless of their story, we all got along great and that helped the situation tremendously. It was common for us to sit outside in the sun and practice our wheelchair wheelies. We would flirt with the cafeteria ladies and try to get extra pudding from them. Some of the guys liked to smoke weed as it can help with muscle spasms, so I would hang with them while they got high. They would giggle about the idea of dinosaurs using catheters and suppositories. Weird stuff.

I tried smoking weed with them but it didn't help me at all, so I stayed away from it.

I had work to do.

I started spending fifteen minutes every morning and every night working on moving my toes. I don't know how to describe it, but I just stared at them with no neurological connection trying to get them to move. It was as if I looked at someone else's feet and said to my brain "Move those toes!" and then nothing happened.

It was a weird feeling, and very frustrating. But I kept working away.

Therapy continued with basic tasks such as transferring to the wheelchair on my own, dressing myself, and putting on my own Velcro shoes. It took a bit of time to learn the transfer process, but once I got it I was out in my chair wheeling around the facility as much as I could.

Despite at times not having any movement, there were times where involuntary movement drove me insane. Many people with an SCI get muscle spasms in their legs, arms, or even their bladder depending on their injury level. Your muscles just start to twitch at any point for an indefinite period of time until they decide to stop.

It's the brain trying to send or receive information and the interruption at the injury level causes your body to freak out. To this day I still have muscle spasms. They are more controllable now, but back then spasms could make or break my day. They are intense.

Another muscle spasm male SCI patients get is growing an erection all day long. In most cases you would always be thankful it goes up more than it stays down. When you're wearing jogging pants all the time for ease of life, this can get in the way.

On the plus side, when I got injured I was dating a girl. She came down to visit and the first thing I told her was to not worry about me. She was not on the hook. We had been dating but weren't serious enough that either of us expected to necessarily be together forever. The beauty of that situation though was I got to have sex in my hospital bed. Twice.

I wish you could experience the feeling. Because of the nerve damage, I had some tingling sensations running through my body. It was like the CN Tower in Toronto being lit up with fireworks. It was insane and one of the best shows ever.

Not only was there excitement from the fireworks show, there was also the thrill of trying not to get caught. We had three beds beside us with nurses walking in and out. It took some work to keep the bed from squeaking and waking the neighbors.

As the weeks wore on, I continued to work on my toes. I kept trying over and over to will them to movement, until one day on week six, I saw a flicker in my right big toe.

"Did I just do that!?"

I thought it might have been a muscle spasm. Twice more it flickered but I still wasn't sure. I went to sleep and thought I would try again in the morning.

The next day I didn't say anything to anyone. I just got in my commode chair and hopped into the shower. I ran hot water onto my foot to loosen up the muscles and then all of a sudden, on command, I got my right big toe to move multiple times.

"Nurse! Come here! Come quickly! You've got to see this!!"

A nurse dashed in to watch me move my toe. She didn't have the level of excitement I had hoped for, but it didn't matter. This definitely meant "Game on".

After that day it took me one more week to wiggle another toe. Then another week to wiggle a few more toes. And on week eight, I got both ankles to move. My progress was literally step by step, one toe at time.

I get asked all the time at my speaking engagements "How did you do it? How did you ever learn to walk again?" This was exactly how I did it.

Just like any goal in life, it begins with a baby step and you build from there. At the beginning when you have an idea it may take a lot of convincing for people to believe in you. You have to be the one to prove to them that it's possible. When you start out on that journey like I did, you are full of excitement and ready to take on the world. You feel like it's going to be a linear path to success and hurdles will fall away from you before they get in your way.

It takes fighting through doubt until you finally get that taste of success, and then you have to build on that. Gain momentum. Keep fighting and don't quit. There's always more work to do and learn. My mom used to have a quote posted on the refrigerator at home. It read "You have to learn from the mistakes of others, because you won't live long enough to make them all yourself."

When I got into Lyndhurst people kept telling me that the first year of recovery is the biggest window of opportunity. That's the greatest chance to succeed in walking again as the nerves try to wake up and the body heals, so you have to make the most of it.

I knew that on days when I was waking up early to get to my physio appointments and I would pass my friends in their rooms still sleeping I had an advantage over them. It wasn't a race against anyone but myself, but every day I was getting results and saw others staying in the same old place because they weren't willing to fight.

Now that I had moved some toes, I was even more determined to make my time at Lyndhurst count. Once I got my ankles to move I would work on flexing them every day. I did the same with my toes. I would throw on my leg braces and hit the parallel bars as much as my body would allow to build up the strength and wake up my nerves again.

I knew that if I wanted to be the comeback story that I needed to have a comeback video. The FMX pros had someone to film all the time, but I didn't. Since Casey was working I decided to film myself. I would set my camera down on something or ask someone to film me just so I could capture footage early on. Today, this has paid dividends. I used some footage in my TSN piece and clips are also available to watch on my website.

Despite my progress, there were days where I still doubted myself. My bowel and bladder were still not working. I used catheters every day to pee. Bowel routines were sometimes for an hour or more in the shower. The whole grueling process involved suppositories, laxatives, and over thirty pills a day. These things often weighed on my mind more than the walking part.

These are the things people don't talk about behind the scenes that really make life challenging in a chair.

Despite all this, my time at Lyndhurst was honestly one of the absolute most favorite times my life. At the exact same time it being one of my worst, learning how to walk again at the age of twenty three was truly incredible.

I felt like I had the joy of experiencing life all over again. I was getting a second chance to be here and was old enough to understand what opportunity I had in front of me. I dreamed of making a comeback just like many other riders do. As Joe Rogan would say, I wanted to be the hero of my own movie.

The progress of going from nothing to feeling a little bit, to wiggling a toe and then my ankles, brought joy to every day. I couldn't wait to get up and see what I could accomplish next.

To me, entrepreneurship feels like that. When you are doing what you love, it's not a task to get out of bed. You look forward to the day, so much in fact that you will be disappointed when you have to go to sleep.

When it was time to leave therapy, it was difficult to give my body rest. I wanted to work so hard and work my muscles twenty four hours straight if it meant I could walk sooner. But life doesn't work that way. You have to learn to have patience.

Nowadays I understand my body more so it's a lot more manageable. I choose my time wisely because I know that I have limitations.

During recovery, I was determined to give it my all. There was no way I wouldn't get better just because I didn't try. I thrived on the knowledge that I was one of the people making the most progress in the facility.

I didn't press on to get recognition from others as much as I wanted to see what was possible. What's possible when you give something your all? What's possible when you don't waste a day, show up every time you have a chance, and make every minute count?

That's what I love. I want to see what's possible, for myself first, and then show others that they can do the same.

Six years old in grade one.

My hockey photo from when I was 10 years old.

Dad and I celebrating our 16th and 46th birthdays together.

My first dirtbike jump ever.

Performing a superman seat grab.

Performing a nac nac over a 75 foot jump in British Columbia.

Family time in the hospital after Dad had his injury.

Signing autographs for kids at my first ever jump show.

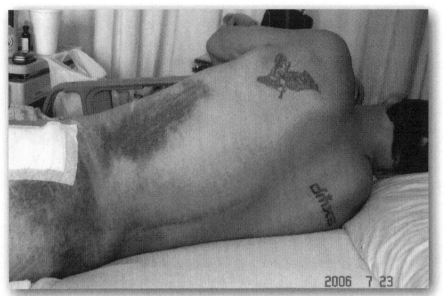

Eight days after my crash.

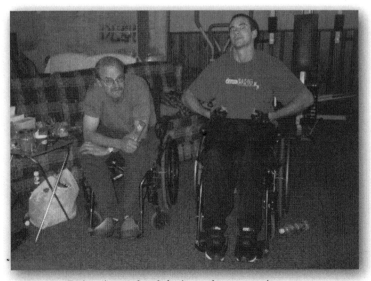

Being in a wheelchair at the same time as
my dad was the most bizarre feeling.

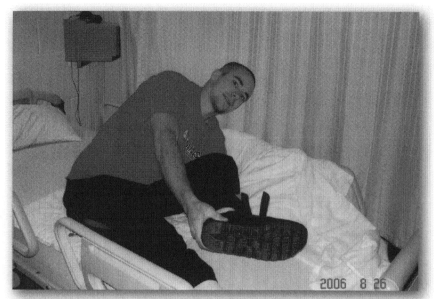

In the beginning of recovery even small steps like putting on your own velcro shoes becomes a huge accomplishment.

I was fortunate to have so many great friends visit me while in rehab at Lyndhurst Rehabilitation Institue, Toronto.

I wish my dad chose to live so he could see
what I have accomplished today. Suicide is not the answer
to your problems. (Photo credit: Dennis Romanin)

My GG, "Groovy Granny", has always been my
biggest supporter next to my mom.

Winning the 2013 World Championships in Goyang, South Korea.

Charging ahead while playing in the 2014
Paralympics in Sochi, Russia.
(Photo credit: Matthew Murnaghan /
Canadian Paralympic Committee)

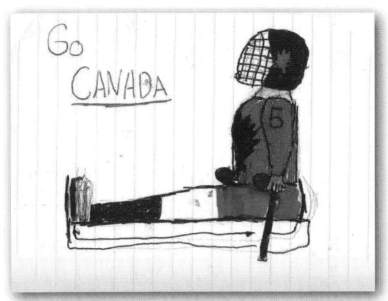

One of the drawings I received from a student
while competing in Sochi.

A look at the benches in sledge hockey. The boards
are clear so you can see the play going on. The bench
surface is ice, flush with the playing surface.

Hanging with my family in Sochi.

Celebrating a goal with my teammates Dominic Larocque and Marc Dorion.
(Photo credit: Matthew Murnaghan / Canadian Paralympic Committee)

Two of the friendliest volunteers I met while competing in Sochi.

Derek Whitson and I receiving our medals.

Team Canada receiving our Paralympic bronze medals.
(Photo credit: Matthew Murnaghan / Canadian Paralympic Committee)

It feels amazing to accomplish your goals and
dreams. I encourage you to go live yours.

CHAPTER 11

Three Visitors That Changed My Life

■ ■ ■

THANKFULLY IN ADDITION TO HAVING a great group of friends around Lyndhurst to hang out with, family and friends came to see me. I was at my worst, and their taking the time to visit me sure brought a smile to my days.

I've never been one to count on people but it was super nice when someone would show up. I felt like I was disconnected from the outside world so when someone showed up to take me out to dinner or go for a walk around the facility, it really helped put things back into perspective.

Most of the guys who initially came to visit me at Sunnybrook hospital kept in touch in their own way. Some visited on their own, others came with a buddy. Some phoned.

Tim, however, never showed up again. That hurt a lot. I expected him to be there. I still hadn't gotten over our relationship breaking up as badly as it had, and hoped that maybe he'd come around. Other than a couple of emails I don't remember ever hearing from him again.

The visitors who had the biggest impact were the ones I never would have expected.

Lube and I didn't have that close of a relationship in my opinion. He was always at the track with me, and had been there the weekend before my crash when I called Tim and found out he was riding at the Molson Indy. Truthfully though, I never gave much time to the guy.

When I got hurt Lube called me more than any of my other friends did. Lube showed up with cookies his mom had baked. He took the magazine ad I had from my sponsor and got it blown up into a hundred posters for me to hand out. I never had anything printed to autograph at that point and that in itself was like a dream come true.

In addition to those few things, Lube did another unbelievable favour. I had $1000 worth of t-shirts printed for Underground FMX right before my crash. I sold about ten to fifteen shirts at the initial Lindsay jump show but all my cash was sitting in that cardboard box.

Lube took that box of t-shirts and sold them like crazy, making my money back for me. Then he showed up to my hospital room and handed me back $1000 in cash! I was amazed. I honestly felt embarrassed inside. Lube had the biggest heart and my first impression of him had been a wrong one. He has forever changed my perception of the impact we make on others and who your true friends really are. It made me want to be a better friend too.

Because of Lube I always try to treat people fairly. It's not easy, but the old saying of "Never judge a book by its cover" pops into my head a lot more often now. We never know how far what we do or say will go. Our actions impact others much more than we think.

Lube taught me a lot about having empathy for others. I don't feel inside like I always want to drop what I'm doing for people. I like being on my path and pursuing my own goals. Lube has helped me pause when the thought runs through my mind of helping others and consider what a few minutes of my time could mean to someone else. He helped me realize that just a few minutes of my time can change a life forever. I feel an obligation to serve and help others now, because of what others have done for me.

The next visitor who blew me away while I was at Lyndhurst was Curt. Curt and I went to BDSS high school together for a couple years but did not consider each other friends. We were more like acquaintances.

Curt was a drug dealer and was at the top of his game. He had money. He had women. Curt always had new clothes. He had wheels, a pager, rode a skateboard, and knew how to shred a guitar or a set of drums. We partied together but were never close. I didn't really care for the guy. He was an asshole and he'd admit it.

After I was in Lyndhurst for a few weeks I got a call from Curt. It was kind of out of the blue. My first thought was *how the hell did you get my phone number and why are you calling me?* I wasn't exactly excited.

Curt asked if he could come visit me and catch up. At first I hesitated. I really appreciated the thought of anyone wanting to come see me, but I also didn't want someone I didn't like bothering me. I thought I might have trouble getting him to leave. Curt was really enthusiastic about visiting me though, so I consented. I really didn't expect him to show up.

The following week he was supposed to come after dinner at 7:00pm. I was in the cafeteria eating and so resentful of the thought he might actually show, I ate slower to avoid returning to my room.

When I finally did roll down the hallway I saw this guy at the end of the hall, seated on a couch. He was wearing a collared shirt, a cadet hat, and beige pants. It was Curt.

"Hey Remps! How's it going brother!?"

"Ahh, good man. How are you?"

"Man, I have so much to fill you in on. Let's grab a seat."

Curt proceeded to fill me in. His last few years had been his own crazy ride. Curt continued to sell drugs. He met some guys at Wasaga Beach in Ontario and partied with them for over a year, doing bigger drug deals all the time.

One day while making a deal Curt was meeting these guys in a parking lot at a hockey arena for a $20,000 deal of ecstasy, mushrooms, and pot. Just as the deal went down and the exchange of money happened, SWAT teams ran over the snowbanks and surrounded the vehicle. Curt was headed to Jail.

While on probation he'd had a job doing roofing estimates. One day while walking around the house carrying the ladder he struck power lines and electrocuted himself. Emergency responders pronounced him to be without a heartbeat, but were able to revive him. Newly brought back to life, he continued to await trial.

Due to the electrocution, his lawyer got him a reduced sentence citing psychological issues, and he received eighteen months of house arrest instead of a jail sentence. While locked in his basement Curt got into self-help books and began turning his life around. He paid off his $30,000 debt in drug and lawyer fees and now owned three rental properties while continuing to do roofing.

"How the hell did you do this Curt?"

"I'll tell ya what Remps. Next time I come I'll bring you the tapes I used and maybe it can help you in your life. They're 1987 cassette tapes titled Unleash the Power Within."

A week later Curt showed up with the tapes. Over the next several months this became the kick start to my own addiction to self-improvement. Curt's ridiculous turnaround story and great success was impossible to ignore. I thought there might be something in those tapes that could help me down the road.

The third visitor that changed my life was Tracy. Tracy doesn't have a crazy story behind her. We met in January of 2006, just six months before I had my back injury. Tracy worked as an assistant at the chiropractic office in Orangeville. Ironically, I had been going there for treatment of a sore back. I had back pain so bad before my injury that I used to wake up and immediately take Tylenol before breakfast, then again consecutively every four hours throughout the day.

Tracy's office had been very helpful in treating me. Since I couldn't afford to pay the full price they offered me a position helping do administrative work. I applied the computer skills I had learned in school, and helped pay for them to fix my back. It's a little bit ironic that six months later I snapped it in half.

Tracy came to visit me in Lyndhurst once. When she came I was happy to see her. She was cool and I appreciated that she cared to come say hi.

When she arrived she had in her hands a pen and a few notebooks. They were the cheap kind you would easily find at the dollar store. "What are those for?" I asked.

"They're empty. In case you want to write something down." She said handing them to me.

"Alright, well thank you." I took them with a smile, thinking *"When the hell am I ever going to write a journal entry? I have never journaled before."*

I placed the books to the side and we continued our visit.

One night when I had nothing else to do I decided to pick up a journal and start writing. Something Curt had said during his visit was on my mind and I wrote it down on my first page.

I scrawled the title, How Can I Use This? I then circled it and drew lines outwards from it to other word bubbles.

Curt had told me to think of how I can use my circumstance to improve things in my life, and also to remember C.A.N.I. which stood for Constant And Never-ending Improvement.

Beneath the title How Can I Use This, I wrote the first point. I can use this circumstance to improve my relationship with my dad. I had always wanted a better relationship with him, but didn't know how or where to start. I actually thought that now since we are both in wheelchairs this may bring us closer together.

I wrote these thoughts down and started to expand on them. What I learned about starting to journal is the power one gains from it. I started to notice the small things in life that were exciting like seeing my friends, flirting with a cute girl, enjoying the sun, doing a favour for someone to see them smile, or simply just being alive.

We get so caught up in the little things that bother us that we often overlook the small things that bring us joy. In rehab those small things for me also meant wiggling my toes, having a good bowel movement, and walking a couple extra feet each day. When I flip through the pages from my time in rehab they are almost all good memories. My time there was precious and so were the memories.

Thank you to all of my friends who came by and visited me, called, wrote an email or messaged me during my time at Lyndhurst. Each of those meant so much.

There isn't much you can do wrong to show someone you care when they are knocked down. As I think of how I've gotten to where I am today, I want to visit someone at Lyndhurst and help brighten their day. More than that, I dream of helping people on a grand scale and it's my responsibility to serve others just as people have helped serve me.

CHAPTER 12

Home Is Where The Hurt Is

■ ■ ■

As my time started to wind down at Lyndhurst I had to start thinking about moving home. For many injured patients this can be a very troubling and stressful time. Often the timing depended on whether or not they had received any insurance coverage for their accident and if their home would be modified for wheelchair accessibility.

There was definitely irony that I was moving home to a place that was already wheelchair accessible. My house had two elevators in it and a wheelchair accessible shower. I didn't go through any stress that way. What stressed me the most was thinking about being locked up in my house with Dad all day.

Dad had continued to be depressed after his accident and had such a victim mentality about his injury that he was more miserable than ever. Now that I was injured in the worst way possible -exactly how he had envisioned - I just knew that we were going to butt heads.

Thankfully because of my lawyer, I was able to get some insurance coverage. I was lucky because I didn't have insurance on my dirt bike, but through the no-fault insurance policy I had coverage through my pickup truck. Doctors had deemed me catastrophically impaired which meant I received money for attendant care and for rehab. This was pretty much the best case scenario.

In my first week back home therapists were already lined up to see me and keep the ball rolling. Suzanne was the first to arrive. She walked in through my front door and immediately started asking me questions.

"Move your leg over here. Ok. Now raise your... Nope! Start again. Do this, now lift your leg... nope! Stop. Okay, try wiggling your toes. Now take a step... hold on."

I was getting angry. I was already not myself because of the gross amount of pills I was taking on a daily basis. The medication had caused my ears to become super sensitive to sound and I would get irritated by the smallest little thing. Something as simple as a fork and knife scraping on a plate sounded like nails on a chalk board.

"How come you aren't listening to her?" dad piped up. "I told him he's been doing too much. The spasms are probably because of that. You should go to bed."

I lost it. Right in front of Suzanne, on the very first visit, I started yelling at dad to shut up and asked her to leave. I couldn't deal with the physical struggle and mentally I knew that it was only going to get worse with Dad around.

Next I was introduced to Stephen. Stephen helped me on days that Suzanne couldn't attend and did more basic work versus intricate movements. Stephen and I would spend two or three sessions a week lying on the floor trying to get my legs stronger.

Gravity to this day can still be my worst enemy. I fought so hard, for years trying to raise my leg up in the sky. I have strength in my quads to kick and lift, but on my side, no way. It still is excruciating to try and lift my leg with my hip flexor muscle. I hate it.

There were many more days I cried on the floor with Stephen just trying to get my leg up off the ground. Since that first day with Suzanne, I always did therapy in the basement away from Dad so he didn't have the chance to say anything to me.

Obviously, it was inevitable we were going to spend time together. Mom would wake up and go to work. Rebecca was off somewhere. By the time I got out of bed Dad was already up and in the kitchen listening to the depressing AM Radio.

I don't even think it's possible to describe to you how it made me feel. Dad would sit all day at the kitchen table reading the newspaper and talk about all the bad things in the world while listening to the most monotone voice that crackled from the radio into the room. Dad would repeat this process day in and day out.

I was angry before I even ate breakfast, because the more you listen to that type of garbage, the more it permeates your brain. Dad was doing nothing to help himself, only digging a deeper hole.

It took no time at all before we started to fight. There were a few things said by Dad that I will never forget, and to this day can't comprehend why they were even said.

Once we were fighting about something small and it escalated into an argument about how Dad has it the worst and we (the family) have nothing to worry about. Even before my injury Dad would tell us all how his injury didn't impact the lives of anyone else but his own.

"Seriously? Do you think that having my father in a wheelchair, shitting himself in our house, crying himself to sleep, and seeing him depressed and gambling his money away every single day doesn't affect me!?"

"Oh come on. That's my hobby and it's none of your business."

"Well Dad, it kind of is my business. You just can't see it. You're wasting your money and you're dragging us all down."

He didn't care.

At one point, he said, "You have no idea what it's like to be in my shoes!" I was sitting in my wheelchair across the table from him when he said it.

"How the hell can you say that! I am right here, in a chair beside you! I can't shit properly and I piss out of a catheter. What do you mean I have no idea?"

"Well you can stand, so that's totally different."

"Yeah I can stand, but don't tell me I have no idea what it's like to live in your shoes. I'm not out of this mess yet. I'm fucked just as bad as you are, but I'm busting my ass to recover and you aren't helping me at all."

I seriously felt like Dad had resentment towards me that I was able to walk and he couldn't. There were never words of encouragement.

Never a "Great job today" or "Hey, you're looking pretty good." It was always resentment, put downs, or some other way to communicate that I was somehow not good enough.

I admit I was no peach to deal with either. I had my own moods and disorders. The pills I was taking were seriously messing with me. At dinner for example, just the sound of a utensil touching a dinner plate was loud enough to send me over the edge. Oxycodone made my ears incredibly sensitive to noise. I would break down in tears while eating and would have to finish supper later on my own.

I fought depression too, especially during those first few months back home. Yes, I had everything lined up with accessibility, but I had no money, no income replacement benefits from a technicality in my policy, and now my life came to a complete stop.

"What am I doing here?" I thought.

My life felt like a mess. I didn't know who I was anymore. I didn't feel confident that things were going to work out. I failed at my motocross business and now I started telling myself that I wasn't a good rider.

"I never should have crashed at the show that day."

I had no idea what I was going to do with my life, who was going to want me, where I was going to get a job, or if I would ever really be able to walk again. Some people suggested that I consider going back to school to get a new education and brush up on things. There was no way I could consider school when it was a big enough chore to make it out of bed.

I wish Dad and I could have started working out together, or maybe doing some kind of hobby even from our chairs. Perhaps we could have helped each other through our depression together but we couldn't seem to get beyond asking each other to pass the salt before we started brewing under our skin.

I wish things had been different.

When you have a life changing injury there is no instruction manual. You literally have to take things as they come and just deal with them. There's no predicting how you or other people are going to react.

When it does happen though, you have a choice about how you are going to handle it.

My dad continued to choose a cynical, resentful, and pessimistic mentality of a victim. While our family was around we tried everything we could to help the guy, but he just didn't want to change. I knew how badly I didn't want to be this way and this is at the core of why I am the way I am. I didn't want to be like my Dad.

When I had to go through what he went through, I knew that I didn't want to drive away my friends. I knew that I didn't want to develop negative habits. I knew that I didn't want to lock myself up inside and give up. You are capable of living a fulfilling life, even after SCI. You just have to make the effort and figure it out. Nobody is going to do it for you.

When you encounter challenges in your life, don't wallow in self-pity. Figure out how you can overcome those challenges. Do whatever it takes. Read books, listen to podcasts, find someone who has been through your struggles and learn from them. There is enough information out there that rarely in life will you be going through something that no one has dealt with before. There are countless stories of people who struggled with the same challenges as you might be facing who have overcame them.

Two of my favorite quotes ever are W. Mitchell's statement "It's not what happens to you, it's what you do about it.", and Booker T. Washington's declaration that "Success is to be measured not so much by the position that one has reached in life but as by the obstacles which he has had to overcome to succeed."

You have to be the one to make the decision to move on with your life and accept responsibility for your situation. Life isn't fair and that's a good thing. It gives you the opportunity to always reach higher, perhaps reinvent yourself. Nobody wants to endure hardship, but we all have to. Resilience is built when we face our fears and attack the situation head on. If you succumb to your fears you will never overcome them.

Trust me, you are capable of much more than you think.

CHAPTER 13

Time For A Comeback

■ ■ ■

I COULDN'T STAND BEING AT home around my dad, always being dragged down. I needed to move. Thankfully my rehab team had gotten me a vehicle with hand controls so that would help with my independence.

We had a very hard time in the beginning and luckily came across Bethlehem Place in St. Catharines (today it has been renamed to Genesis Court). It was a brand new community building and had one wheelchair accessible apartment left. I threw down my application as fast as I could. I knew this was the spot.

Bethlehem Place had a very mixed group of people. There were single moms, beaten women, retirees, students, and people with disabilities. It truly was community housing.

Soon after I moved in I started meeting the people. There were some good and some bad. My first week there a crackhead came to my door. She stood there, teetering back and forth, with a face full of zits and she didn't even know the name of who she was looking for. I was so grossed out. Not a great start...

I met some lovely people like the retired couple down the hall. Bruce and Mary were in their eighties and had been married for over sixty years. They were so incredibly sweet. Mary eventually became like a grandmother to me, even helping me iron my clothes at times. We chatted about life and how it was hard for me to adjust from being a twenty three year old living full speed ahead and then coming to a complete stop.

Mary said, "Well I can imagine! We've had sixty years to slow down our pace and we still aren't used to it!"

She was a hoot.

My pad quickly turned into the sickest bachelor pad ever. I had my snowboard hanging off the ceiling. My dirt bike jerseys were lined up above the couch. I had my TV and Play Station set up with Guitar Hero and room to wheel around as I continued to learn how to walk.

At this point the wheelchair wasn't necessary for everything. I could take small steps around the apartment, but still had to use it for things like grocery shopping, touring the mall, and even going to the gym. If I was going more than fifty feet or standing for more than 10-20 minutes, I needed my chair.

The apartment really helped me regain some independence. I needed my mom to help me with things like cleaning and grocery shopping, but knowing that I could soon look after myself made me feel like a man again. I wanted to cook my own meals. I wanted to get dressed myself. I wanted to get to the gym on my own and workout without someone watching over me.

The move did all these things and one more. I didn't like that I had to run away from Dad but there was so much less negative energy when I wasn't around him. I felt like I could start focusing on moving forward at a faster pace. I don't remember Dad ever coming over to see the place. We just chatted on the phone once in a while and Mom would keep each of us in the loop as things went on.

The one year anniversary of my accident was approaching. Time flew by and before I knew it the thought of getting back on my bike was becoming a reality. This sounds absolutely crazy, but even if I couldn't walk very well I was sure that I could ride. I wasn't the least bit scared about getting back on my bike. It was literally something I dreamed about ever since the day I got hurt. It's in my blood, and I love it.

I had just ditched the wheelchair to use walking canes full time and that was enough to get me out to the sand pits with my friends.

On July 15th, 2007 exactly one year to the day, I celebrated with friends, counting down to 2:05pm, the time that I had crashed and kicked my bike over. Thirty of my friends showed up with a keg of beer and a barbeque. Casey came to film the whole day. We created a video capturing it all and it was seriously just like old times. I can't say just how excited and thankful I truly was for both my friends and my recovery. I felt like anything was possible and I still had more work to do.

While this was going on, there was a lot of other stuff going on. No one knew how our family was collapsing.

Throughout the years following my dad's injury he developed a serious gambling addiction in addition to his depression. The issue was bad enough that it was starting to drive my mom away. Mom would sometimes share stories of their car rides home. Dad would tell her about how many different ways he would think about suicide and how easy it would be. He said he didn't want to live anymore but he had been saying that since the day he got hurt. It was horrible, and Mom had finally had enough.

I sat down with her, my sister, and my grandmother and we talked it out. We all knew that Mom wanted to leave but had to do it safely. My dad never hurt my mom before, but Mom felt he was so unstable that she didn't want to say something and then go to sleep. One day she moved out while he was at the casino.

I must emphasize that this is something our family fully supported. We saw how Dad under-appreciated Mom. We tried as hard as we could to help him get back to life but he chose to play the victim role for so long it was clear that nothing was going to change. After five years it was time for Mom to move on.

After that Dad started trying everything he could to get Mom back, but she wasn't running home so quickly. Dad's behavior made me uncomfortable. He started speaking like a man I'd never met in my life. Words like "I love you" and "I'm sorry" hadn't existed in my dad's vocabulary for years. Now they were the basis of his conversation.

I wasn't expecting it, but he and I had a heart to heart after my anniversary ride. Dad told me he was proud of me and that he really loved Mom. I said I would try to help, but things weren't going to change overnight just because he did.

It was really, really tough.

Dad had had a long time to get over his injury and start getting active again. He did do some things like stain the front deck. He did a lot of body work in the driveway on the pickup truck and the boat. He had even gardened when he could. I could see it was difficult for him to bend over in his wheelchair and do that. I was proud of him for that, but after five years his attitude was still that he was a victim.

When Mom left, it was a wake-up call for Dad. It just seemed like the call was too late. Dad quit smoking, washed his own laundry, and wrote her love letters just so he could prove his independence. He even wheeled his chair to Mom's work one day. She worked one kilometre away, and his knuckles were raw and bleeding when he arrived just to tell her how desperately he wanted her back.

But it was just too much of a shock all at once and Mom knew well enough that real change happens over time, not overnight.

I began feeling like my messed up life was normal. I didn't know what it was like anymore to have a normal family and believed I never would. It made more sense to me to get used to the way things were and just remember the good times from years before. I never knew how good I had it.

I remembered my dad bragging about all those years when I was a child that I didn't know how lucky I really was.

"You have a roof over your head." He'd say, "You have family dinners with food on the table. You have a bed to sleep in and you have clothes. You don't know how lucky you really are."

Even more importantly, when I was a child, I had a tight family. But that was a long time ago.

After chatting on the phone with Dad one day, he was talking about suicide again. He told me he didn't know how he would continue on without Mom in his life. Rebecca and I had both moved out, so he wondered who or what else he had to live for. Blaming others or laying guilt on them only causes more problems. I wished he would be strong and accept responsibility.

It was always a fight to protect my mind. I had so many things going on that there was no telling what would happen next. I felt like I was in a war for my sanity, and I was ready to stay in this war as long as things kept moving forward. I was a solider.

Even soldiers get knocked down though, and I was about to get some big news.

CHAPTER 14

Getting The Wind Knocked Out Of Your Sail

■ ■ ■

MY FMX RAMPS HAD FINALLY, finally arrived. It was such a shitty feeling to still be in rehab, writing a $5000 check for something I was likely never going to use. I thought about continuing Underground FMX and putting on shows, but I was in no shape to do that and I really needed to pay off my debt. I decided to try to sell this one-off $15,000 piece of machinery.

By God's grace, I found someone who wanted to buy one and agreed on $12,500. On July 27th, 2007, after this ramp had sat around for nearly a year, I arrived at my buddy's farm up in Orangeville to prepare the ramp for pickup.

I was on the side of the road when I got the call.

"Kevin!" It was Carly, the neighbor who lived across the street from my dad. She was upset and crying. "I just want you to know that no matter what happens we are here for you."

"What!?" I had no idea what was going on.

"There are cop cars all around the house." she said, "What's going on!?"

"I don't know -" I was stunned. "I'll find out."

I hung up, and quickly called my mom at work.

"Hi Mom." She sounded calm but I knew something was wrong. "Carly just called and said there are cops at the house. Do you know what's going on?"

"Dad just called and said he cut the locks off the gun case and found three bullets that we didn't know about. He has a loaded gun. He asked me if I am definitely not coming back and I said that I wasn't. He said then he has no other reason to live and that he was going to shoot himself. … I had to hang up before I heard a gunshot."

"Are you okay Mom?"

"Yeah." she said, "I'll call you back when I know more."

At this point, I didn't freak out. Like I said, this was my kind of normal despite this time Dad apparently had an actual gun in hand. I carried on helping prep the ramp. It wasn't long before I got another phone call. It was Mom, and this time she was crying hysterically.

"Well… he finally did it -" she stammered between sobs, "he ended it."

Dad shot himself in the chest using his own hunting rifle. At that moment everything went still.

It was over. After five years of hearing my Dad talk about it, he finally did it. That dreadful thought was now over.

That might sound cruel, but for us it was like The Boy Who Cried Wolf. The threats had been there for years, gnawing at us and making us wonder. Now there would be no more joking around and keeping us on edge. For me personally, I felt like I could finally relax. It was scary to feel relieved.

I headed into town to pick up my sister in Toronto. When I arrived we gave each other a big, long hug and then got back in my truck to drive home. We drove in complete silence. We spoke no words, and shed few tears. I think we were both just numb inside.

Rebecca had finally started to build a connection with Dad since Mom left. They never had a great relationship either but they were definitely started healing some wounds as Dad started to open up and realize what he had. And now he was gone. I felt very sorry for her.

When we arrived at my parents' house, Mom and Grandma were waiting for us. We gathered together inside the front door and gave each other a long hug. I still felt so numb inside.

We briefly spoke with a police officer who informed us that Dad's body and all of his hunting guns had been removed. I don't remember much else about what he said, but I do remember he asked if we needed

Family Services to come speak with us. We figured that after all we had already been through, we would be fine. The officer left and we closed the front door behind him.

The house was quiet, and none of us knew what to say or do next. The whole thing felt like we were in a movie, being played in slow motion. My chest and stomach felt empty.

To this day I have no idea why we weren't offered anything else for support. No one told us what the situation was downstairs so we just headed that way to find out for ourselves.

I rounded the corner of our laundry room and made the turn to head down into the basement. I led the family. At the bottom of the steps laid Dad's wheelchair. The cushion was on the ground, and as I got closer I could see the pool of blood on the seat. Dad's reaching stick was also there, and the portable phone was lying on the ground.

Mom broke out in tears. "This is all my fault! I killed Dad!"

It was such a horrible, shitty feeling. We all went into the basement rec room to cry together.

When we'd finished, we turned our attention to the mess that needed cleaning. The carpet had been heavily stained and there were droplets of blood on the wall. We couldn't leave it like that. No one had said they were coming back to clean it up. So we cleaned it up.

We grabbed a warm bucket of water and some rags out of the garage. Mom and Rebecca went upstairs while Grandma and I took care of things downstairs. I cut away the stained area of the carpet and threw it in the trash. We used several buckets of water to wash down the wall and wheelchair.

While wiping the portable phone dry, I thought it was probably weird that this is normal. Flushing red water down the drain was just another day in the life of Kevin Rempel. In a way I couldn't believe I was doing what I was doing. But then again, I could.

I don't remember much of the days that followed. Mom and Rebecca slept at Grandma's house and I went home to my bed. After settling down for a few days, plans for the funeral service commenced.

Mom and I discussed what we should put on Dad's tombstone. We decided on using an image of a deer. Regardless of how Dad's injury had happened, he still had loved hunting his whole life. We also had engraved the Toronto Maple Leafs logo because my dad was a die hard Leafs fan.

The Town of Lincoln had been home to Dad. He had worked for the town for decades. When the time came for his visitation, there was a lineup out the door of the funeral home for the entire two hours on both days. I couldn't see it for myself because I wasn't able to leave the lineup since we were chatting with everyone.

So many of Dad's friends showed up. I remember feeling a sense of joy knowing that my dad had impacted this many people. I could feel the sense of loss in the community knowing that he was gone.

In preparation for the funeral my sister and I went to church where she practiced a song on the piano that Dad had loved to hear her play.

The day of the funeral I felt pretty calm. I sat beside my sister while she played that song on the piano. In practice, she was having a difficult time concentrating. She cried as she played. For some reason I didn't. But, when I got to the podium to read the eulogy, I finally broke down. Reading my dad's eulogy was the hardest thing ever.

"I don't know why this happened to you." I read, "I feel so sorry for you and wish it would have been different. I hope you feel no pain anymore."

When I left the podium the emotions settled down again, but in that moment I felt deep pity for what had happened to him, and such deep sadness that he didn't get a better ending to his retirement. I felt the hopelessness of it. Maybe it was a little taste of the hopelessness Dad had felt all those years.

I wasn't looking for closure, but I guess putting Dad to rest did bring some. The whole family was relieved that Dad would no longer be suffering with his injury.

Living with a death in the family, especially when caused by suicide, can be a touchy subject for some. Having gone through this experience makes it worthwhile to talk about because I know it can help others. I know my dad isn't the only one who ever felt like things were hopeless and who ever wanted to end their suffering.

Suicide is an escape from your current reality but will bring you no closer to happiness. You may solve problems in your mind, but you are creating more problems for others. It impacts people around you more than you know. What's worse, is that it opens the door for others to do the same. You don't want to start a history of this happening in your family.

To this day I still believe that Dad could be living a great life. My dad had the ability to take care of himself, but he had such a mental block he was convinced that life was over, that there wasn't anything else worth living for and he needed to end it.

If you feel like that – like life is not worth living - know that suicide is a permanent solution to a temporary problem. You must stay positive and maintain focus knowing that at some point things will get better. You must keep fighting, my friend, to see that day.

CHAPTER 15

Regrouping In Costa Rica

■ ■ ■

AFTER THE BURIAL THERE WAS some time where the dust needed to settle. Figuring out Dad's affairs was mainly straight forward since Mom was deemed the survivor. I was able to help her with the funeral proceedings but she took care of the the will, Dad's pension, and other legalities.

Back in my apartment I couldn't keep from continuously thinking about how times had changed so much from just five years before when we had been a normal family.

Back then my biggest concerns were what course I would take in school, resentment of chores I had to do, and that family meals were boring.

Now my thoughts were very different. I wondered how the hell we went from that to Dad being paralyzed and then me breaking my back one year later. How did we end up with Mom having both a husband and son in wheelchairs? I learned how to walk again, and then Dad committed suicide. ...What the heck is all that?

The whole family was looking to get away from it all. We wanted to simply move on in life. The worst part was over now and there was still so much out there to do.

Mom and Dad had bought into a time share several years prior, but we had never used it. It was approaching expiry, and so Mom asked us all one day,

"Hey, would you guys like to go away to Costa Rica!?"

We looked at each other, and couldn't think of a single good reason not to go. So we all agreed and began planning for our first family vacation in over ten years.

Way back when my sister and I were little, the family vacationed annually up north in Ontario. They were usually fishing trips for Dad, but we kids had a blast running around the cottages and lakes.

When I was around thirteen, Dad announced a new vacation plan.

"We won't be going back to the cottage next year..... because..." he paused dramatically, and widened his eyes, "...we want to save up so we can take you kids to Disneyland!!"

"Yay!" Rebecca and I were jumping up and down.

But Disneyland never happened. As time went on, even if we had still wanted to go to Disneyland, Dad's gambling habit took away any idea of us spending a few thousand dollars for a week-long trip.

This trip to Costa Rica was going to be the Disneyland trip we never had.

As we prepared and packed we were gearing up for some pretty warm weather. We pretty much expected blue skies and the hot sun beaming down on us at all times.

When we arrived we were taken by a shuttle from the airport to the resort. Our drive was beautiful and we saw some of the most gorgeous sights of lush green valleys. Upon arrival at the resort we checked in and soon made our way to a patio. Before long, we started to feel a few rain drops.

Within a matter of minutes it was pouring rain and it was in that moment we learned we had just gone to visit Costa Rica during rainy season. In a place like Costa Rica, the rain is not like our rain up here in Ontario, Canada. Their rain comes down in short bursts, and it comes down hard. One minute you can be sunbathing and scorching hot, and the next minute you can be running for cover and questioning if you'll step back outside that day. The only consistency about the weather was that you would never know what the sky would do.

We ran back inside as the rain came pouring down. Palm trees were blowing in the wind and animals were running for cover. We stood on our balcony watching it all and began to laugh.

"Well!" Grandma laughed, "Looks like we will be doing all of our activities in the rain, eh!?"

Rebecca, Mom, and I all giggled at the thought. We agreed nothing was going to stop us from having a good time. On the plus side, rain season meant there was hardly anyone else there, so all activities were open for booking and we had many options.

The first activity we chose was white water rafting. I had never been in a real raft scenario before and neither had my 69 year old grandma, or "GG" as she liked to be called, which stands for Groovy Granny. She is one of the most adventurous, kick ass grandmas you will ever meet and she's usually down for just about anything.

After all we had been through, playing it safe didn't matter as much as having fun and living in the moment. We were going to do this.

As we headed down the river in the pouring rain, our guide told us about the different classes of rapids. Class one and two rapids were fairly easy, but we would soon approach a class three rapid called The Devils Mouth.

"Hold on!" he yelled. We crashed and tossed around the water. In a split second, a wall of water confronted us and sent the raft nearly straight up in the air! We all lost our seating. GG flew overboard.

"Grandma!" I yelled.

The guide stayed calm, while we tried to right the raft. We all looked at each other on the raft. We had just lost Dad. Would we lose Grandma too?

If music would have started to play, the moment called for the theme song from Rocky. GG hung onto the side of the boat like a military survivor. Just like our guide instructed us to do, when she'd fallen out, she'd grabbed the rope lining the boat, and saved herself from floating away.

Now drained of energy, she was limp like a dead fish as our guide pulled her into the boat. She started to cough up water. When she finally got herself composed, the guide asked her,

"How was it!?"

"It was WET!" she smiled, "Let's carry on!"

What a kick ass grandma.

We had so much fun. Whether it was horseback riding, zip lining through the rainforest, or ATV riding along the mountains, we did it all and we did it in the rain. Just seeing new scenery and getting to spend so much time giggling and laughing was all the therapy we needed.

One evening, we all sat in the kitchen of our hotel room and looked over to each other.

"This is nice. It's nice to not be stressing anymore."

We felt like we were getting on with our lives. Being away from anyone who knew our story let us be ourselves. The trip definitely brought us closer together.

We continued to party a few nights and got drunk as a family. We had never done that before. GG was already pretty badass in my opinion, but after the white water rafting excursion she definitely put herself in a league of her own. Rebecca and I joked around about meeting some sexy Costa Ricans to marry and bring back to Canada but didn't find any.

More important than anything was for Mom to know that we had her back. She was loved.

What happened back home was not her fault. Dad had made the decision to end things and we had an opportunity to either dwell on it, or move on. We were all moving on.

I kept journaling throughout these times and also continued to grow spiritually. I dabbled back and forth trying to get into the Bible and find reasons for why everything was happening, but nothing seemed to work for me. Journaling allowed me to keep in touch with my spiritual side. It was as though I had a relationship with someone who understood me. Each entry gave me the chance to share my thoughts like praying does. As a result, I was able to rest my head peacefully at night.

By the time we left Costa Rica it felt like things were going to be okay. We had a ton of laughs and were going home with hangovers, near death experiences, and memories that would last a lifetime.

We also felt like we had the opportunity for a new beginning and were determined to make the rest of our lives count. That realization influenced my sister's decision to move to Australia. It's also the reason I continue to strive after so many big goals today. The trip wasn't a turning point per say, but a much needed reminder of how tight our family still was.

CHAPTER 16

Fighting The Demons

■ ■ ■

UPON RETURNING HOME FROM COSTA Rica it was back to the grind for me. I had to continue therapy and was actually looking forward to it.

Vacations are nice to relax, but my body will struggle if I don't do some specific exercises and stretch regularly. The gym is important to keep functioning smoothly and without pain. Plus, when all you do is rehab, the gym is a great place to escape to and get out of the house.

While I was there one day I saw a flyer on the wall advertising wheelchair basketball. Basketball wasn't my thing but I thought I'd give it a shot. It was more interesting than wheelchair racing, the only disabled sport I knew of at the time.

The team was called the Brock Penguins, hosted by Brock University. They were a small group, but it was a lot of fun to play around in the chairs. It was there I met another guy with a spinal cord injury named Charlie.

"You've got to try sledge hockey, bro. It's pretty sick." He told me, "You sit down and haul yourself around using two sticks. They have spikes on the end, plus you get to hit people!"

I laughed. "That sounds pretty fun!"

Sledge hockey is the Paralympic version of hockey where you play sitting down. You sit in a sled or "sledge" and pull yourself around the rink with your arms. The rules of hockey are the same. You just can't T-bone another player. It is primarily played by people with disabilities, though at a house league level able bodied people can play too. Disability is a requirement however at the Paralympics.

Common athlete disabilities include those who were either born with it or acquired it later on in life. Spina Bifida, cerebral palsy, amputation and spinal cord injuries make up the majority of the disability types in the sport.

Because I'd played hockey as a kid, this was a lot easier to picture playing than basketball. Charlie told me of a local sledge team, the Niagara Thunderblades, so I signed up for my first ice time just a few weeks later. The start of the season was not far away.

As soon as I got on the ice I knew this was what I wanted to do. I was falling over from my left to my right side, and just like a Timbit hockey player I went full steam ahead until I learned that I didn't know how to turn.

"BANG!"

I slammed into the end boards so hard it felt like I dislocated my hips. Regardless, this was the start to my new passion.

Meanwhile back at my apartment I had started heading in another direction with where I was spending my time.

One day I walked out to my truck and found a note on the seat. It read, "You're cute, you should call me!"

I thought, "What the hell. Sounds like an adventure." and dialed the number. It turned out to be a girl who lived on the floor below me. Her name was Karen.

Karen was a good looking girl, and also an ex-stripper. She was a little rough looking from partying and doing drugs for many years, but she was cool, and so we became close friends.

In the beginning, I kept a safe distance from her because while I continued to do proper things like eat healthy, get proper sleep and exercise when I had the chance, Karen wanted to sit at home all day to smoke cigarettes or weed. Those two things were entirely counter-productive to my trying to get better.

Karen also had two kids from two different dads. One of those dads was in jail.

As time passed, I started to fall for her. I began altering my daily schedule to accommodate what she wanted to do and before I knew it I was throwing all the progress I had made out the window.

I started skipping gym sessions. Protein shakes were replaced with pizza and beer. I liked to have an occasional puff once in a while but now I was buying my own packs of cigarettes and getting high on a weekly basis.

It was nobody's fault but my own. I was getting myself in this mess. I knew she was bad news from the start, which was why I initially kept my distance. She had brief moments where she said she was quitting smoking because she wanted to make me proud, but as soon as we became a couple she lit up again.

Karen also had friends who loved the same things she did, so whenever we would go somewhere, it was to get high. Even when we'd go to the park, we'd smoke up while the kids played on the swing set.

I have nothing against smoking if that's your thing to do, but it's not for me. I also didn't want it in my relationship. I knew this was only going to bring me down, and fast.

Adding to all of these elements, in rehab we were experimenting with the idea of injecting Botox into my legs for help with the muscle spasms. Muscle spasms are caused by your brain not recognizing the signals being sent up and down your spinal cord, causing your muscles to tighten and cramp up. Spasms can be intense and sometimes painful.

Botox was supposed to alleviate these cramps, but the second treatment completely wiped out any existing strength I had left in my calves. I needed three months for the Botox to wear off, and several more to regain the strength I had just lost overnight.

After having worked my way back to walking, I was back in the wheelchair and becoming seriously depressed.

I reconnected with a friend from Lyndhurst so we could chat about our struggles and possibly help each other. He came down for the night. We smoked a joint by the beach and caught up about what our lives had become. Unfortunately, this evening led to one of my scariest experiences ever.

My friend gave me a Percocet to help with my back pain. I thought there was no harm in it so I took one that evening and another the next day.

The next morning when I tried to stand up I felt like I was floating. My legs were working better, my back hurt less, and I could move around without pain. I felt like Percocet was the answer and I went to my doctor to get them prescribed.

I took two to three pills a day and felt that I was progressing in my recovery because I felt better. The truth however is that in a matter of two weeks I completely fell off the face of the earth. No longer was I going to the gym. I was too tired to. I stopped buying groceries because I didn't have the energy to go to the store. My appetite was gone and drinking became more frequent.

I started telling myself things like "My friends are too busy to hang out. I'd be bothering them if I call.", so I stopped hanging out and stayed home all the time because that made the most sense to me. I was ok I thought, so I was better off being alone.

Percocet was taking control of me and I had no idea.

As 2:00am approached, I couldn't stop staring at my ceiling. All the lights were on in my apartment and an empty case of beer lay on the counter. Five Finger Death Punch was blasting loudly over the stereo in my living room and inside my head all I could keep hearing was "Take another pill. You want it. You need it. Just do it, man. What's the harm?"

I had taken a pill just one hour before. They are supposed to be spaced out every four hours. I didn't need another pill.

"Just do it." My mind said it over and over again. "Just do it."

I walked over to the kitchen counter.

As I stood there tears began to trickle down my face. I had never thought about suicide until that point but it was now becoming a reality. I didn't know how to handle this situation anymore and thoughts about it started to go through my mind.

"Your dad did it, so why don't you too?"

"No one would blame you. You've been through a lot."

"Yeah, it's the easy way out but if you get it over with now you won't have to suffer anymore."

"Nobody cares anyway. You'd be doing them a favour."

I saw the knife block and reached for a knife. The voices kept getting louder and louder as I pointed that knife towards my chest.

Finally, as I felt the tip gently touch my t-shirt I knew I was too close to the edge, and I screamed.

"FUUUUUCK!!!!!!!"

Slamming the knife down into the counter, the blade broke off and went flying. I dropped the handle and started to cry.

"There's no way I'm going out like this. Suicide is not the answer to my problems!"

I'd battled through enough tragedy in my life. I would not take the easy way out like my dad did. I had more fight left in me and this would not be the way I ended my story.

Ever since my dad died, Mom had always said that suicide is a permanent solution to a temporary problem. I resolved to never forget that.

There, still standing at the kitchen counter, I took one pill so I could fall asleep. The next morning I called my buddy John.

"John, I need help dude. I know you've had a lot of friends who have dealt with this stuff. What's going on man? I don't do this shit."

"You're addicted, man. The drugs are powerful. You need to quit as soon as possible and get better."

"Should I wean myself off?"

"Just go cold turkey. Don't mess around. There will be a few days where you will go through withdrawals but just fight through it and know that it's the addiction talking and not your real voice. Call me if you need me."

I went home after that and flushed all my pills down the toilet. That stuff needed to be out of my apartment as soon as possible.

The next few days were the worst. I had cravings for a Percocet and sometimes would take Tylenol 3 to suppress the cravings, but my goal was to stay as far away from prescription drugs as possible. My goal was to just take Advil or acetaminophen as needed.

Negative thoughts would still fill my head so I did what John said to do and called him. Sometimes a small chat would help put things back in perspective, that I was going through a tough time and better days were on the horizon. I knew that this demon was big and I couldn't let my ego get in the way and prevent me from accepting help.

I can't even begin to tell you how scary that was for me. It feels embarrassing dealing with depression and suicidal thoughts, but that's the truth. I was that close to doing what my dad did.

It took me a long time to get back on my feet. I fought that addiction and those thoughts on an everyday basis for months, but let me share with you some things I did immediately that changed my direction the very next day.

"You can't change your destination overnight, but you can change your direction." - Jim Rohn

By focusing on those things that you can control you give yourself the best chance possible of dealing with the demons.

First, I bought healthy food. It seems so basic, but one of the things that was constantly dragging me down was that I was always feeling sluggish. Eating fruit and vegetables, and drinking lots of water cleans the system out, and it gave me the best chance to feel good. Feeling good helps me do good.

I also exercised. The very next day I got back to the gym. Exercising releases endorphins into the brain and helps us feel more energetic and positive, and also helps move food through your digestive tract which is crucial to someone living with an SCI.

I also called up my friends and got out of the apartment. Life in a wheelchair left me spending way too much time inside. I needed to be around people again. I needed to see there was more to life that just rehab. A fun evening with friends could be as important as a gym session. The mental balance is necessary. One can't just work all the time.

I also got proper sleep. I had been staying up to 2:00am every night and sleeping in until almost noon. Morning appointments had been impossible and half the day's sun was wasted. I got my butt out of bed and built a solid routine. I woke up every day at the same time and would listen to a playlist I made of positive YouTube videos while I showered and cooked a healthy breakfast.

In addition to those four basic tasks, I also developed some other strong habits to keep myself positive on a regular basis.

I created a vision board. It seems cheesy but it actually works. It is important to create a vision and image in your mind of what you want to be, where you want to live, what you want to do, and where you want to go. But having it on paper makes it that much more real.

I created a quote board and hung it in the bathroom. Each time I heard or read something I liked, I would write it on my quote board. I put the board over my toilet because I go there six times a day. That's six chances to memorize that information and really get it into my brain.

I also got back to journaling. At a time when lots of confusing thoughts washed through my mind, it helped tremendously to get them all out on paper and really see what was going on inside my brain. It didn't take much time and each day I could reflect on what was good in my life and not what was bad. Journaling, like most everything else listed here, is free and something that I have control over to help get me out of the gutter.

Just like anything in life there comes a point where someone or something is no longer needed and you have to make the decision to move on.

After two years with the Niagara Thunderblades and one year with Sledge Team Ontario, I knew I wanted to make the next step to Team Canada. I had to go all in on my next dream.

The best players in Canada were who I needed to surround myself with so I decided to get out of St. Catharines. I began setting things in motion, first to move, then to pursue training for the 2014 Paralympics in Sochi, Russia.

CHAPTER 17

Let' s Try Things Again

■ ■ ■

I WORKED TOWARD TWO GOALS: I wanted to financially set myself up for the future. I also wanted to become part of Team Canada.

Without really knowing where I would go, I gave notice to move out of Genesis Court. I was excited because even if I didn't know where I was going, I knew that putting myself in a "must move" scenario was the best motivation.

You can't wait for the timing to be perfect to move forward.

Where I would live was uncertain, but an issue that had been in limbo with my insurance was finally settling. Blessed is each of us who are fortunate enough to have insurance take care of us.

As I was reaching a plateau in my recovery, both rehab and insurance staff needed to make the decision about whether they should continue looking after me, or if they should just cut me a check for the remainder of my coverage, and let me take care of myself. They consulted with me too, and involved me in the decision making process.

There's a feeling of security to be under their umbrella. But it was like living at my parents' house in that I needed to continually ask for approval to do things. I wanted to make my own decisions.

One of the first things I did when I was offered a payout was talk to my rehab team. They had been around long enough to see patients take the cash, blow it all within a few years, and be left in the dust with no way of looking after themselves. Their recommendation was to put it away securely for the next several years, withdrawing only small monthly payments.

Then I called Curt who had been in the rental business for five years, and I asked him what he would do.

"Take the cash!" Curt said. "Do you have any idea how much more you can earn if you invest it yourself?"

At the time I didn't, but we started to play with the numbers a bit more and it was starting to make sense.

I thought buying a rental property could set me off in the right direction. I knew that I had to make some smart decisions from this day forward since returning to a normal life wasn't practical anymore. I was walking, but to this day I can't stand up or sit down for long periods of time without getting really uncomfortable. Just making it through the day can be challenging. I needed to build a future that I could sustain living on my terms with my injury.

Being told I can't or shouldn't do something really makes me want to prove I can do it. When I told people about my rental property plan, they objected.

"What if you get bad tenants?"

"What if you lose your money?"

That made me pretty determined to find a way to succeed. It was just like the doctors telling me I'd likely never walk again. I would find a way.

I also had resting in the back of my mind what life was like for those guys on the job site who were in their fifties and sixties. They hadn't invested their money properly, and were pissed off to still be working.

My parents had done well with making smart money decisions but they'd lived a very frugal life. Everything those Tony Robbins tapes talked about was about thinking in terms of abundance instead of thinking about scarcity. I needed to reshape how I thought about money.

Knowing that Curt went from a broke drug dealer to full time employed person and multiple property owner, I knew this was a guy who had the bigger vision.

Curt began by offering me books to read like Rich Dad, Poor Dad. As I grew my mind with confidence, the task of becoming a landlord became less overwhelming.

Curt also assured me that while going through this process, if I encountered any challenges I would have him to call on as a mentor for advice. He'd already been through hell with tenants destroying places and not paying rent, and had battled other money troubles. If he'd survived through the worst then there really was nothing to fear.

It wasn't an overnight decision. It took several days of feeling sick to my stomach. I felt like I had to decide on the rest of my life. Should I take the settlement and run, or should I play it safe with modest pay checks and have a planned, modest lifestyle.

Underground FMX may have failed, but I wanted to try the business thing again. I opted for a balanced approach taking 75% in cash and investing the other 25% away in long term growth.

As I began looking for a house I knew two things: I needed to be as close to the Greater Toronto Area as possible and I needed to find a place with a rental ready to go.

The hockey arenas of the best players on Team Canada were found in Oakville, Mississauga, Newmarket, and Barrie. Because I couldn't afford to move all the way to Oakville, I settled in the town of Dundas, right beside Hamilton.

Dundas wasn't originally on my radar. It's so small I didn't even know it existed. What was really key is that not only did it have a basement ready to rent out, I was right beside McMaster University, a Sport Canada supported training center. This meant I could get discounted physiotherapy and massage treatments along with top notch training at a high performance facility.

If I wanted to be great, I had to do everything I could to set myself up for success. The 2014 Sochi Paralympics were only four years away and I had lots of work to do.

I moved to Dundas in the summer of 2010, shortly after the Vancouver Paralympics ended. Team Canada had finished the games with a disappointing finish in fourth place. I remember watching the games and feeling for the guys because there was a lot of pressure on them to do well. Playing in your home country in the Paralympics was one thing, but they had the added pressure of trying to win "triple gold" as the women's and men's teams had both won gold just weeks prior.

Knowing several players on the team were considering retiring after Vancouver, I thought there was a good chance that a few spots would open up at the start of next season.

While boxes were being unpacked and renovations began, I attended as many ice times as I could in preparation for September's selection camp. I got on the ice with guys like Brad Bowden, Greg Westlake, and Billy Bridges. These were the top guys on the team and a great measuring stick to gauge my skill level.

I know now that there was quite a difference in skills and ability compared to those guys, but at the time I felt like I wasn't too far off. It takes that level of confidence to get to the next level. The guys were looking for some new energy to bring to the dressing room and I felt like I had some value to bring.

A few weeks before selection camp I got the email invitation to attend. I was pumped!

We headed up to Ottawa at the Canadian Forces Base Petawawa and spent a few days getting acquainted with each other. We endured many ice and gym sessions, and even took part in some fun military training exercises.

The daily grind was hard but I went to bed each night feeling confident that everything I had put in up to that point was paying off. I also had a feeling that I made the right decisions getting on the ice with Team Canada players. By the time I'd arrived at camp, it just felt like another regular skate with the boys.

On the last day of camp we waited in our dorm rooms as the coaching staff brought each player in one by one to give them the news. I waited anxiously as I could hear guys close their door and head down the hallway.

At one point I thought I heard a bus leave from the front of the building. I wasn't certain, but that may have been the other guys leaving to go home. Players who made the team were going to stay a few extra days.

"Kevin Rempel, you're next." as my team manager Adam Crockatt called my name.

I headed down the hallway and took a seat in front of head coach Mike Mondin, assistant coach Billy McGuigan, and Adam.

"How did your glove hold up?" Mike asked.

I had ripped the palm of my hockey glove during a practice and stitched it up using a needle and thread. Good thing GG had taught me how to do that.

"It held up pretty good!" I said. "I know you guys didn't think it would but my grandma taught me how to sew. She knows her stuff."

"Well that's awesome, Kevin. Good stuff. I have some news for you though. You won't need to sew your own gloves anymore because from now on you'll be getting them for free. You just made Team Canada."

"WOO HOOO!!!!!! HELL YEAH!!!" Every muscle in my body tensed up with excitement. I was clenching my fists and a huge smile spread across my face. I tried to keep my cool in front of everyone but inside I felt like I put my head through the ceiling I had jumped so high.

All the hard work had paid off. After becoming an FMX rider and learning how to walk again, now dream number three had just come alive and I was now on my way to being a part of Canadian history.

How awesome is that?

I felt like that pile of hard times was about to pass and I was on my way to something greater. It was so cool to make the phone call to my mom and tell her.

"I made it Mom!" I smiled into the phone.

She was at work at the time and started jumping and down, screaming with excitement. I can't begin to tell you how proud I was of what I had accomplished. I was ecstatic to make her proud after all that she had been through.

Now that I made the team, my training would step up to a whole new level.

After calling Mom, I raced to my calendar and - as any Olympic athlete would do - I counted the days until Sochi. We were just under four years away from competing and I knew that if I had any plans to stay on this team, I had a lot of work to do.

CHAPTER 18

Doing The Team Thing

■ ■ ■

HOLDING OUR TRAINING CAMP AT Canadian Forces Base Petawawa was one of the best things that could have happened to me as a part of this team. I have always heard about guys dreaming of putting on the Canadian jersey and representing our country. That reality never really sunk in for me until selection camp.

While we were there, soldiers at Petawawa shared stories about how they'd lost friends due to war. They told us what it was like to live life on the front line knowing they were defending our freedom. They had families back at home. They had children.

It made me think about how much sacrifice they go through to endure rigorous training, much harder and severely disciplined than we have to deal with, just to have the chance to go to war. They were real fighters and it is because of them I really feel the pride and honor of what it means to don a Canadian jersey.

As a Team Canada member, when I played I no longer represented myself. I represented my friends, my family, and everyone back at home who cheered me on. There was a feeling of unity in the belief that through encouragement and empowerment we can all succeed together.

My time there really made me proud being Canadian.

The first year on the team was really exciting. We had so much positive energy from the new players, and the members that had competed in Vancouver's 2010 Olympics had finished fourth and they were looking for redemption.

I wanted to contribute to the team and one of the hardest things I had to deal with was leaving my ego at the door.

I like being in the limelight. That's why sports like motocross, BMX, and skateboarding appeal to me so much. I like the extreme aspect and I also like to be the center of attention.

I like counting on myself. I know that when I tell myself to do something it gets done. When it comes time to perform there is nobody else to count on but me. If I win, I did it. If I fail, I'm responsible for that too. There is nobody else to blame.

Being on a team meant I had to put all of that stuff aside and focus on what was good for everyone else, not just me. I needed to remember that when I didn't perform at my best, not only do I let myself down, I let the team down. A team can't win if its members play with ego. That behavior will act like a cancer inside the dressing room and people will resent each other. Things won't function properly and the team won't be successful.

This applies even away from the rink. Sometimes it's not just about winning a game. Dinner is just as important.

One time while playing in Japan we had an off day and decided to go for a walk around the city of Nagano. We left the hotel as a team and said we would all stay within a reasonable distance from the hotel. After an hour we could head back together or buddy up. We decided to meet at the hotel for dinner in one hour.

My teammate Derek said he would hang with me so we decided to try to get a quick haircut at a Japanese salon. To be honest, the idea of trying to flirt in Japanese with a hair stylist was more exciting than the haircut itself.

Not only did the haircut take longer than we expected, but we were lost as soon as we walked out of that salon door. We had fifteen minutes to make it back and had no idea where to go. Derek and I started to walk a little faster and take some turns we weren't sure of.

Adam, our team manager, had a cell phone but I didn't know his number or even where we were. If I turned my phone off of airplane mode I knew my bill would skyrocket.

We had no other choice though, so I did it. As soon as I switched my phone on, it started ringing loudly with incoming texts from back home. I ignored them, and found our hotel on Google maps. Derek and I made it back, walking in twenty minutes late for dinner.

The guys were standing in the foyer, waiting for us. I decided to start the conversation by putting my foot in my mouth.

"We went the right way but you gave us the wrong directions, Adam!"

"Wait. Whose fault is it?" Adam asked me.

"But you said…" Before I could finish my sentence Adam cut me off.

"I said what?"

I realized my mistake right away.

"Sorry. It's our fault. I mean, it's my fault. I shouldn't have gotten lost. Sorry guys."

There's that taking responsibility lesson again. The guys weren't too upset with me, they were just hungry. I learned two things through that experience.

One, it was amazing that the team will stick together and wait for you for dinner.

Two, don't be late for dinner.

We lived through a few crazy things as a team. We were in Japan during the 2011 Tsunami, for example.

We had been playing a hockey game at the Big Hat arena in Nagano when it initially happened. I was one of the guys on the ice skating when the ref blew the whistle. Nothing happened in the play that warranted a whistle, so I joined my teammates over by the benches and asked what was going on.

"Look up at the Jumbotron. We just felt an earthquake." someone said.

"What?" I looked up and saw 50,000 pounds swaying back and forth over center ice.

"That thing shouldn't be moving. I guess no more face offs, huh?"

So, when things stopped moving, we resumed play.

When we flipped on the TV back at the hotel, we found out just how bad things really were. Living through a major worldwide event like that brought the Team Canada experience to a whole new level.

Over the course of the next two years we travelled to South Korea during nuclear war threats, the Olympics in Russia had terrorist threats, and we missed our Hockey Canada Gala in 2013 due to the flooding which evacuated the city of Calgary.

It really has been a wild ride. And we weathered it all as a team.

In 2012 we entered the world championships with high hopes of winning. The previous year we had won the Sledge Hockey Challenge, beating our prime competitors, the USA team. We had also won all of our games that season. I felt like we were unbeatable!

In the first period of the world championship finals against the USA team, we came out flat. From the opening face-off we struggled to keep the puck out of our zone. USA got up two goals in the first period and there was some deflation in the dressing room during the first intermission. We got one goal back in the third but in the end, lost 3-1. Our dressing room was quiet after the game. We were so disappointed.

I couldn't understand what went wrong. I felt like we had done everything we could to prepare and we still lost. The excellent season was over. None of those other wins mattered, just the final game at World Championships did. It's unfortunate but that's the reality, even at the Olympics. We don't have a regular season of games. We only play in tournaments so you need to make every game be your best game.

The following year we were considered the underdogs. USA had the title and there was a calm feeling amongst our teammates because we knew we had nothing to lose. I think this may have been the first time I felt that on the ice. It's thrilling because there is so much power built up behind it. It's almost like you walk around stone cold in the face but inside you are smiling ear to ear because you know you're about to explode. We were ready for battle.

In the 2013 World Championships the game was the complete opposite scenario. This time we had the puck down in their end the whole game. I remember crushing guys with solid body checks, making some great plays, and really connecting with my line mates Marc Dorion and Dominic Larocque. It was tough to score but during the second period our defensemen Graeme Murray lobbed a puck on net. It took a funny bounce that redirected it around USA's goalie, Steve Cash.

That was enough for us to hold onto the win. And, though it wasn't pretty, we had finally won a major championship together as a team. Forever I can look back and say that I was part of a gold medal, championship hockey team with Team Canada.

The championship ring we wore afterward represented many hours on the ice and in the gym. Another entire book could be written on just that. As a team you go through so much anguish, practice, and patience with each other that putting the team first is the only way this could have been accomplished. I particularly remember the positive atmosphere and guys being unselfish with line changes. That was one of the biggest clinchers to our success.

I feel deeply proud to wear that championship ring and to have earned it with a great group of guys. That year was one to remember.

We only had one thing left to do and that was win at the 2014 Paralympics in Sochi, Russia.

Playing on the world stage in world championships is one thing. Playing in the Paralympics meant TV coverage, numerous loud screaming fans, and pressure that normally wouldn't be there. It was time to get our minds right as the next twelve months were going to be intense.

One of the biggest lessons I learned heading into the final twelve months of the journey was to let the singers sing and the dancers dance. It was a phrase our coach Mike Modin said to us right before we headed into that gold medal game of 2013 Worlds.

He meant that, if you look at a team like a theatre performance, it needs a star. Someone needs to take the front stage, being the face of everything. They often get the glory for successes but also take the most heat for failures. Regardless if that person is a star or not, they would not be able to perform if they didn't have someone to open the Lucasain, operate the lights, and usher people to their seats. There are so many different roles involved.

On the ice we had to consider what our role was and perform in that role to the best of our ability in order for the team to succeed.

We have guys who are great at penalty killing but don't get power play time. Their stature and skill level is best for short movements and blocking shots and they excel at that. We have guys who are great on the power play unit and work well together. Usually it's the top five guys on the team and they have set positions based on their own skill level. Third line players may not get as much ice time as they want and their job may be to simply not get scored on while the first line guys get a rest.

We each have a job to do out there and we need to do it well so everything works together as one unit, one team.

What is my job? I know that I am out there to have a physical presence. I am one of the biggest guys on the team standing 6'1" tall, 205lbs. I have good hands and great puck control. I like going into the corners and getting the puck out to our point or into the slot. I also know that I am not a guy who will out-maneuver a double amputee or blow past him with speed. It's not to say that it can't be done, but I need to focus on my strengths, play my role, and let my teammates take care of their job.

In my five years on the team I had some pretty good stats. The first thing I want to do though is acknowledge my teammates. If it wasn't for them getting me that puck or making smart plays so I could win the race to go dig it out of the corner, I wouldn't have those numbers. Brad Bowden, Billy Bridges, and Greg Westlake spent the most time helping me over the years to become the best I can be. If I didn't have their mentorship on the team, I wouldn't have been as successful.

CHAPTER 19

Sochi

■ ■ ■

ONCE THE 2013 WORLD CHAMPIONSHIPS were over, Hockey Canada rescheduled the gala in Calgary that had been cancelled due to the flooding so we could receive our Stanley Cup sized championship rings. We had an amazing time at the gala but then it was time to return focus on the next task at hand. The Paralympics would creep up on us quickly.

I made a few adjustments in my training program to meet the end goal.

First I had two of my teammates, Derek Whitson and Tyler McGregor, move in with me. This gave them a place to live closer to Oakville from their hometowns and it helped keep me on track.

I also had to leave McMaster University where I had trained for the three years prior. That was hard for me to do. They had really become a family to me, but I needed to do whatever it took for our team to be the best.

My teammates and I had been discussing the idea of working out at a new gym, Beyond The Next Level in Oakville (BTNL). BTNL was located in the Canlan hockey rink we frequented and was an ideal set up that allowed us to work out and then hop directly onto the ice after. They have a killer change room inside the gym, a hot tub, and all the amenities needed to do all our hockey training in one place.

Since Hockey Canada could only support getting the men's and women's hockey teams centralized, we essentially took it upon ourselves to centralize as many players on our team as we could.

Nearly eight of the seventeen guys on the team got together on a regular basis and we were able to establish a tempo that gave any sledge hockey player a run for their money.

We ran both gym workouts and ice sessions four to five days a week. We established a strong mentality by supporting each other so that not a single rep was left undone.

Our endurance was becoming so good that we sometimes had full ice scrimmages for ninety minutes or more and barely took any breaks. We were in the zone and it was awesome!

At this time I kept reflecting back on how far I had come physically. I remember thinking about what it felt like to weigh a skinny 175lbs and how I had come back to a healthy, strong 205lbs. The idea of what a body can do when one puts in the work is absolutely astonishing.

Your body can break down, become skinny or fat, and with hard work it can also be transformed into a machine.

Even my teammates who live with spina bifida, cerebral palsy, or who are missing a leg will absolutely blow you away with what they can do. Not only did we have guys that could shoot a hockey puck with one hand better than most people with two hands, there are guys without legs who have more heart than most people.

Training time was over, and we were ready to leave for the games.

The flight over to Sochi, Russia was nearly eighteen hours long. It took reading a few books and several good playlists but our excitement didn't die down once we landed.

We were the first team to arrive. The gorgeous village laid quietly, seeming to await our presence. Fresh pavement lined the streets. Tall, modern condos stood tall and proud with bright signage that read 'Sochi 2014'. When we saw that, it got us even more excited to play.

People always ask "How was Sochi?", and there were a few things going on, but honestly it wasn't that bad.

For example, we occasionally had a sewer smell in the shower. The power outlets looked rough without covers on them. One of the lamp shades was half full of water from a leak in the ceiling. Other than that things were beautiful.

I mean, I never knew in Russia that water and electricity mixed!

The volunteers were super welcoming. They had so much energy we could barely pass anyone without saying hello. Or in Russian, you would say "Privet!"

We had one week of practice and relaxation to adjust to the time zone change and get familiar with the facilities, and then it was show time.

Opening ceremonies kicked off with a huge performance. It was so cool to walk through the underground tunnel with the rest of the Canadians and then onto the big stage with the whole world watching. The crowd was insanely loud screaming. The fireworks show lit up the Fisht Olympic Stadium ceiling to the most beautiful mix of fire and colors.

For game one we played Sweden and smoked them 10-1. The day after we defeated Norway 4-0 and followed that with a 1-0 victory over the Czech Republic. We had a great preliminary round just as we expected.

Heading into the semi-finals we were expecting USA to also have swept their division. Russia, who had just assembled a sledge hockey team five years prior, had developed world class skills. Russia took game three from USA in the round robin with a 2-1 victory.

That meant we would play against USA in the semis, which was not what we had hoped for. We wanted to see USA in the finals.

For the semi-final game, we had no loss of focus. We had taken time to rest, have our meetings and get treatment on any sore body parts. We did everything we could to prepare for that game.

When the puck dropped the intensity maintained a high pace with every single shift. The endurance we had obtained at BTNL was paying off and the entire team was working well together.

Both teams had chances early on but after just missing a breakaway opportunity in USA's end, USA scored the opening goal. Declan Farmer pushed one through our goalie Corbin Watson and at the 5:49 mark they were on the board.

We battled back hard and got a few shots on net but then again with 56 seconds left to go in the first period Declan scored another. This was not the way we wanted things to go. We had to regroup.

The dressing room talk was positive. We were still very confident we could come back from a two-goal deficit.

Calm your breathing down.
Focus.
Make tape to tape passes.
Let's get back out onto the ice.

As the second period began we had a chance to get back in the game early with a power play, but weren't able to capitalize. The score would remain tied until the third period when USA put one more in our net and after that it was finished. We pushed and pushed, taking chances to trying to get one in the net but couldn't beat USA's goal tender, Steve Cash. We were headed to the bronze medal game.

It was a sad time. The guys were definitely gutted when we knew we for sure weren't going to be playing for gold. The amount of work you put in to get to that game doesn't justify only 45 minutes to play. You want a best of seven series. That, unfortunately, is the nature of the beast when it comes to Paralympics.

It was time to keep our heads held high and come out swinging for the bronze.

Our captain, Greg Westlake, brought our attention to something very valuable. He said, "That bronze medal means a lot. We don't have time to sulk over this loss because we need to still go out and win a medal for our country. If you ask anyone who finished fourth in Vancouver they will all tell you they wished they could have still won a bronze. We have work to do. Let's go."

I wasn't thrilled about it but he was right. Even if bronze isn't the color we had hoped for we couldn't go home empty handed.

The bronze medal game was against Norway. We knew Norway very well from playing them over the years. We knew they could be a force when they wanted to. We had to play smart. We didn't want to let them get the first goal and put us in a corner again.

Period one was scoreless. We maintained control of the puck and had most of the chances. Period two opened up the scoring just 30 seconds in when Brad Bowden lifted a soft backhand through two defenders to put Canada on the board. Billy Bridges soon put a second one in just two minutes later and then another in the third period to seal the bronze medal.

It was bittersweet but certainly something to be proud of. We were now and forever going to be called Paralympic medalists.

Heading back to the arena later that night was exciting and grueling. On one hand, we had the medal to look forward to. On the other hand we couldn't stand the thought of walking into the stadium knowing that the gold medal game was being played, and we were not in it.

We stood in a hallway alongside the rink for the final five minutes as the gold medal game between USA and Russia wound down. As the buzzer went, Team USA was declared the Paralympic gold medalists.

"Fuck" I thought, "That sucks."

I was so angry I actually wanted to punch someone in the face.

Tears swelled up in my eyes as USA cheered and the carpets were rolled out onto the ice. As we were called out I tried to hold back, but when I approached the edge of the ice surface all my sadness went away.

Russian fans were hanging over the side of the railings, asking to take photos and cheering.

"Canada! Canada! Canada!"

There were lights so bright, the carpet was so blue, and for the first time since playing in the arena I could actually pause and make eye contact with everyone in the stands. It was absolutely exciting!

As we walked out onto the ice surface I couldn't help but wave. I felt so thankful for everyone who came to watch us and cheer us on. Although it wasn't for gold, the moment of walking out onto the ice surface to receive a medal for all the hard work was something I had dreamed of for years. I was proud of our accomplishment.

We waited patiently, and as I stood with my teammate Derek Whitson beside me, he pointed out my family in the stands. Mom, GG, and my sister Rebecca had all made the trip overseas to come watch me play. They were there to see firsthand dream number three come to fruition.

The smile didn't go away as the medals were brought onto the ice surface. Derek, #4, was first to receive his. I was #5 and received mine second.

Next to seeing my family in the stands, I have to tell you that the moment that medal was placed around my neck was one of the most real experiences of my life. It is so heavy!

There was a little bit of a drop when it was presented to me, and that weight is just incredible.

I thought, "This is legit. This is no cheaply crafted medal you receive in high school. This is serious... a real Olympic medal!"

As the presentation continued down the line to the rest of my teammates, I had that moment just like in the movies where my whole life flashed before my eyes. I thought back to growing up in Vineland. I remembered being a kid riding around on my BMX bike and my dirt bike hoping to make it big someday.

I thought about going hunting with my dad and the day he had his accident. I reviewed in my mind his injury, his story and then him taking his life. I thought about learning how to walk again and making the hockey team with the glove that I had stitched. And there I was, standing on the world stage receiving a medal on behalf of Canada.

During that last day one of the coolest experiences happened in the village. Many of my teammates told me about trading clothing with other countries to take home a piece of memorabilia. I traded my opening ceremonies jacket for a Czech Republic jacket I really loved. GG in particular was looking for something of her own.

The authentic Sochi jackets in the merchandise store cost $350 CDN and were way too expensive for us to afford. The volunteers who were so incredibly nice throughout the games were begging to have or trade for anything with Canada on it. So at the end of the games I traded my $10 pair of Canadian red mittens for a volunteer's $350 jacket.

I don't think I'm that great at finding bargains but I nailed that one!

I tell everyone that I truly believe Canada was as favored there as the Russia team. Maybe even more. We were so loved and it was very flattering. Thank you to all the volunteers and everyone who helped make that event a success.

As we headed home, people would say things like "Bronze is still good." It didn't sound great when they said it like that, but I sure was proud to have achieved that in my life.

I was also asked, "Don't you wish you had won the gold?" The obvious answer was yes. We didn't play a game or a tournament without expecting to win. Hockey is our game. We are Canadian. We played every game with the desire to win. Losing sucks.

Thinking back to all those days in the gym and scheduling my life around ice time, it feels good to know that I could not have done anything more to perform at my absolute best in Sochi. I didn't let the team down. I didn't let my country down. I didn't let my family and friends down. That is something I can live with.

As I left Sochi I thought life was going to be straight forward. I would come home as a celebrity and all the big networks were going to want to talk to me.

You may not believe this, but I had no intention of going back to the sport after Sochi. I wanted to move to the next thing and go after a speaking career.

I thought the gigs would flow in and my speaking fee would double by demand. Surely a speaking agency would hire me and I would have so much money that an assistant would be necessary to handle it all.

Of course, that would be ideal and nothing about my story is ideal. It's about dealing with the unexpected. What came next hit me like a slap shot to the chest.

CHAPTER 20

The Post Olympic Crash

■ ■ ■

WHEN THE BRONZE MEDAL GAME was over I had gone around the dressing room and congratulated everyone on a job well done. I don't think anyone knew it but in my mind this was my way of saying goodbye.

I had accomplished what I wanted to in hockey, done a four year Olympic cycle and won a medal, so I was ready to move on. Had we not won a medal I would have felt differently. I enjoyed the last bit of time I had in Sochi knowing I could look back and say, "I did that."

The flight home was long and boring. We took a direct flight to Sochi to avoid losing our sleds and luggage, but took three connecting flights on the way home.

When we arrived at Pearson Airport there was an excited and warm welcome. All of our families and friends had gathered outside in the waiting area and cheered loudly as we walked through the doors. We had some fresh autograph cards to sign from the Canadian Paralympic Committee and media coverage was on hand.

My Dundas neighbors were there to greet me as Mom, GG, and Rebecca had stayed in Russia to travel longer. Making our way home, I couldn't help but giggle a little that after all these trips back and forth to Pearson, that this would be my final one as a hockey player. I was excited that the grueling four year Olympic cycle was now over and I could hopefully relax.

The bed was so comfortable that night. Sochi had had twin sized beds and my feet hung off the end every night. At home, I had a king sized bed with three pillows and could spread out if I wanted to. I didn't find it hard to fall asleep.

The first thing I did was park my hockey gear in the garage and tuck it as far away as I could. I didn't plan on touching it any time soon.

Next, I planned a well-deserved vacation to go visit my sister in Perth, Australia. I planned to go for three weeks so I could make the long trip worth it, get some personal time hanging out with her, and really enjoy the warm beautiful weather that Australia has to offer.

When I was there I picked up a book called Millionaire Motivators. The book wasn't that different than other self-help books I'd read, but it was exciting to start thinking again in terms of my potential and what I could do with what I have accomplished in my life.

It was encouraging that while I was away I was getting requests to speak at events. I returned to Canada for the second time in a month and started to go after these gigs. I secured a gig for $3500 and felt like I was going to do some real damage on the speaking circuit. I took on a few schools along the way and even snatched up some banquet events.

I thought I had things figured out.

After a couple of phone calls though, things dried up quickly. I never got another request for a large speaking gig. Instead, I was receiving requests for the same amount I'd made prior to earning the medal.

"Why did I even bother to win this thing?" I wondered. "It's not all about making money, but man, it sure would be nice!"

The world was stoked about me and my story while I was playing, but once the media coverage died down I was yesterday's news. I had heard about this, but it's another thing to experience it.

I tried reaching out to speakers' bureaus but there was nothing but hesitation on the phone.

I felt that my six years of speaking experience didn't count for anything. Today, I get it. In order to get paid more, one needs to bring more value to the marketplace. Simply telling your story is only good for so long, up to a certain level. If you want to earn more money, you have to think about what exactly you leave your audience with.

While this was going on I reconnected with a girl named Amy. We had met the previous summer at a conference. However, she was dating someone at the time so we lost touch. Amy had heard that I recently returned from the Paralympics. She was interested in pursuing her own dream of being an athlete and wanted some advice, so we got together.

During our visit we hit it off again. This time around, she was single so we started dating. Our relationship was going awesome until it was time to make a commitment and she said she wasn't interested. Ending the relationship was an easy mental decision. Emotionally it was very hard.

I was having a hard summer. Paralympics were over. I wasn't planning to go back and play hockey. Speaking engagements were drying up and I wasn't earning any more money. I had spent all the cash I had leading up to Sochi and then anything left over went to my trip to Australia.

I had my house, two rental properties, a brand new truck, a Harley Davidson motorcycle, a world championship ring, a Paralympic Bronze medal, and my health, but I wasn't happy.

I started sinking deep into depression. The truth is, I became suicidal.

I'd rather not tell you this, but it's the truth. If you are proud of me and where I am today, I need you to understand and hear exactly what I went through to get to where I am today. I know I'm not the only one who has struggled with this.

So, my mom and GG came to visit me. They visited often because I had so much trouble trying to get that nasty thought out of my head. I thought about it being the easy way out from my problems, like my dad did.

"What do I have to live for? I feel like I've already accomplished everything I wanted to in my life. I do still want children and a family but it wouldn't even matter now if I left. I can forget about that dream."

We end up going to the Emergency Psychiatric Ward at St. Joseph's Hospital in Hamilton, Ontario. We waited for two hours before getting to see the doctor. When we finally got in, there was one other patient waiting with us. The young man had at least ten slices on each of his forearms from either a razor blade or a knife. They were fresh cuts too.

When Mom, GG, and I went into our private room to speak with the doctor, this boy and his family went into the room beside us. We started chatting, and then just moments later screaming broke out in the next room.

"Fuck you! You told me I wouldn't have to talk about this! I hate you!" and more, and more, and more.

The boy kicked open the door and punched the container of hand sanitizer off the wall before security was called. I stood up and prepared myself for a fight if he came into our room. I didn't know if I was about to have to defend my family. It was getting pretty intense.

When things finally settled down I looked around at the boy, the doctor, Mom, and GG. It was in that exact moment that I snapped out of it and realized I had to figure my shit out and get my life back in order.

We carried on our conversation with the doctor but I was already on my way up. I was determined to get my life back. I need to not only for myself, but so that I can help people like this young man when they're struggling in similar situations.

I realized that looking back on all my experiences in life I have seen both sides of the coin for so many different experiences.

I have lived with my dad who was paralyzed and I have been paralyzed myself.

I have seen someone who committed suicide and I was very close to doing it myself.

I struggled with depression when I didn't have any money. I struggled again when I did.

I have been depressed when I had very little going for me and also when it seemed I had everything going for me.

I didn't know what else there was to experience. I felt like I had lived the life of a hundred men to have gone through so much by the time I was thirty two.

What I can tell you is this, I don't know what you're going through, but we all encounter the same challenges, doubts, and frustrations about it all. You don't need a story like mine to feel depressed. Splitting up with your girlfriend, flunking some tests, missing out on a job, or just not being happy with where you are in life can all be contributing factors to why you aren't happy with where you are right now.

I get it. I've lived it. We all have down days. It's part of human nature. I just want you to know you can take control of the situation.

Here's how I did it.

1) Accept everything.

Accept things for the way that they are. What has happened up until this point doesn't matter. The past is the past and you have the ability to create a new future. Poor decisions may have gotten you into this situation, but from this point on take responsibility for where you are and choose carefully. You can get yourself out of this funk.

2) Get your priorities in order.

Get proper sleep. When I started staying up really late and having inconsistent bed times I would sleep in until late in the day. I would wake up groggy and then the next evening do it all over again because it becomes very difficult to straighten that out.

Start exercising. After the Paralympics ended I stopped going to the gym and getting on the ice. I lasted quite a while in the shape I was in but if you don't use it, you lose it, so that went away pretty quickly. Leg spasms, back pain, and even my digestion got bad. It was all tremendously impacted by my lack of exercise. Getting regular exercise helps me feel good, get out of the house, and function better. We are not made to stay still for so long like we do these days. Get up and go workout!

Eat properly. Now what is "properly"? Personally, I think it's doing what works for you. Enormous amounts of evidence suggest that a healthy diet significantly affects your mood. Living with a spinal cord injury has forced me to pay attention to my diet just so that I can function properly.

Then, being an athlete forced me to take it to another level so that I had enough energy to sustain the level of training I had been at so long.

From my experience it has been proven that you are what you eat. If you are tired, sluggish, sore, and moody, there's a good chance you've been eating poorly. Do the right things and go find some fruit or vegetables. It doesn't sound exciting but it works.

Get out with your friends. Isolation has been one of the biggest demons in my struggle with depression. What I found was that when I became depressed I started hiding. I thought to myself

"Nobody wants to hang out with me. I will only bring them down and they surely have better things to do. I'm doing them a favour by leaving them alone."

This is a load of garbage. If your friends are true friends they will not judge you for the way you are, they will help you. I can tell you that my friends have blown me out of the water with their support when I actually acknowledged that I needed help. They will be happy to help you, if they are your true friends. You know how good it feels to help someone else? Allow your friends the honor and privilege of helping you. Sometimes receiving help is the gift.

Don't have any friends? Next point...

3) Journal.

If you don't have the courage yet to call someone or get out to make new friends, try journaling first. Like I learned in rehab, writing thoughts on paper helps you see what you're actually thinking. Many times I would write my thoughts down and then when I looked back on it a day later I would wonder "Why is it this bad? Is it really this bad? What if I try to find a way to fix it? Is it possible?" Usually things are not as bad as they seem in the moment. We can have others say that to us, but when you see it for yourself it's even more powerful.

4) Reach out for help, then accept help.

This goes a step beyond getting out with your friends. When you're out with friends, make a point to be clear that you need help. I've gone out before and had a good time. My friends were all welcoming to me being there, but if you aren't willing to acknowledge that you really need help then they will never know.

You also need to be very clear when you are asking for help. You can't say "Hey what's up?" and expect anyone, even your closest friends or family to know what you mean. You need to be clear and say something like "Hey, I'm not doing ok. I need help. Please call me.", and then people will know you are serious and it's urgent. Too many times I reached out and wasn't clear, and never got the help I deserved sooner.

Next, once someone offers you help, know that you need to accept it. Not everything is going to work to get out of your funk, but you have to be willing to try things. Find out what works for you by asking for help, then accepting it.

Start before you get to the emergency room. Depression is a silent killer. It can hit you hard after a big event like when a death in the family or a breakup happens. It can also blindside you after a series of small, progressive events finally grow to be too much. The thing is to take action as soon as you feel yourself getting into this state.

I don't like that I had to experience these things in life, but they made me who I am today. If you too can learn from your experiences you will become more aware and then you will catch yourself sooner.

CHAPTER 21

Looking Ahead

■ ■ ■

It was October, and I was getting back on the ice for some exercise to see if I could rediscover the joy of playing hockey. Bryan Sholomicki was a new prospect for the team, and he and I were driving home from Barrie when the conversation became about moving to Toronto.

"I need to be down there for work." Bry said.

"I need to be down there if I want to make this speaking thing happen." I told him. "Want to move to Toronto together?"

"Sure man."

It happened that quickly.

Bry and I started looking for a place and found a gem of a spot within one week. Dundas and McMaster University were home to me, but like many things in life they were there to help me for a period of time and then it was time to move on.

The move to Toronto was one of the best things ever. It was a big leap to leave behind the comfort of a house, a driveway, grass, and great neighbors on a quiet street. However I just loved the energy and passion people had in the city. I admired their drive to make something of themselves. There was an infectious vibe there that made me want to do more and achieve more.

When I gazed out across the city, I thought about how much opportunity Toronto had to offer. I thought about how lucky I was to have made it through all that I had in life, and how I really wanted to leave my mark on this world.

People have asked me, "Do you think you could play another four years until the next Paralympics if you wanted to?"

"Yes. It's not easy, but I believe I can."

"Well, then you should go for it. When you're forty you'll wish you had done it again since you had the chance."

Heading into selection camp I had a 50/50 feeling of wanting to be there. The team was about to undergo some big changes in hopes of claiming that elusive gold from the last two Paralympics. Twice now the sledge team has had an opportunity for "triple gold" in the Olympics with the men's and women's team winning. Neither in Vancouver or Sochi were we able to capitalize.

The 2015 season was tough. So many new faces came and went and despite the progress we made we finished with silver in the World Championships, falling again to the Americans. At the end of the 2016 selection camp I was released from the team.

"What happened?" is the first comment I get from most people.

What I can tell you (if you haven't already guessed) is that my heart wasn't in it any longer and I'm pretty confident that my attitude reflected in my play. I really wanted to continue to see where things were headed with the team and give it another shot, but it was a struggle. No matter how hard I tried I couldn't make the same level of commitment. I found I was forcing myself to show up to the rink, without the heart I used to have to play.

When it gets to that point I believe it is time to move on, and the coaches made the decision for me that I couldn't make myself. It really was a blessing in disguise.

Today, I plan to continue speaking to help others to overcome their own challenges and adversity. I would like to focus on encouraging people with mental health struggles, people living with spinal cord injuries or disabilities, and also build the sport while educating people about sledge hockey.

If we, Canada, expect to keep pace with the Americans and steal some of these gold medals back we need to get more players involved in the sport. We need to create a larger pool of talent to choose from whether it be more double amputees to match speed, previous high calibre hockey players like Tyler McGregor, or develop kids with disabilities from a very young age. Competition worldwide is continually growing.

There are other endeavours I'd like to pursue too. As an athlete, there is work to do to help get our stories noticed and brought in front of large audiences. I said to the International Paralympic Committee two years ago that I wanted to be one of the people in Paralympic sport who made an impact on Paralympians getting sponsored.

Building on that, my days now are filled with continuing to learn what it means to build a brand. Along with the website, I manage all my own social media accounts and work hard at developing strategies for content creation and disbursement.

This book in your hands is just as valuable to me as my bronze medal. This is something that I will be able to share with my family who is alive today, my children who I hope to have someday, and you.

Life truly is about the journey and not the destination.

What I enjoy talking about the most is all the stuff that happened in between dreaming as a kid and standing here today. The medals I've won, the book I've written, my hockey and speaking career are all made possible because of what I went through. Every year I get more excited about the character I've built, relationships I've made, and experiences I've had while trying to succeed. That's why it is important to continue to share my story. The stage is a platform where I can inspire you to live your dreams and keep faith during the difficult times.

On a grand scale though, I would like to grow the game of sledge hockey. I want to leave the sport in a better position than when I came into it. I dream that one day hockey sleds will be for sale in Canadian Tire. I want able-bodied people to get hooked on the sport too, and keep a sled in their garage. I see sledge hockey becoming like ball hockey - another popular version of Canada's favorite game, and something affordable and fun for everyone to play.

If you take one thing away from my story I hope it is this: don't settle. You can do anything you want in life. You are stronger than you know and are capable of anything you set your mind to. Take responsibility for your actions and don't be a victim to your circumstances. Wherever you are in your life, you have the courage necessary to face your fears and live the dream that is eluding you. Do the thing that scares you.

Every one of us has a purpose in life and it requires following your heart through hell and high water to find out exactly what that means for you. Nothing worth achieving will be easy. Find out what drives you to get out of bed in the morning and go after it.

Dedication, hard work, commitment, and perseverance are the muscle that will run your engine. Honesty, integrity, and humility will keep you on track when you feel like leaving your path.

No one can teach you what these all mean. You have to live it for yourself. It is not going to be easy, but I can promise you it will always be worth it.

Q & A: 20 Sledge Hockey Facts

■ ■ ■

TWENTY SLEDGE HOCKEY QUESTIONS ANSWERED

Q. How do you balance on one blade?
We actually play on two blades under our sleds. When we begin playing sledge hockey we have our blades set apart usually 5"-6". Then as we progress in skill level we move them in closer together. Wider blades help us balance but make turning difficult. When our blades are closer together (anywhere from 2" down to 1/4") we can turn sharper and quicker but it is much harder to balance on. You have to find what width works for you and adjust.

Q. How do you move yourself around the ice?
In sledge hockey we have two sticks. We have a left and a right curve so we can stickhandle and shoot both ways. At the bottom of the shaft there are picks. Each pick has six to eight spikes on it, similar to the tip of a figure skate, which allow us to dig into the ice and grab traction. We play sitting down and pull ourselves around the ice surface using our arms. It is extremely tiring!

Q. Who is your biggest competitor?
Just like in women's and men's hockey, U.S.A. was our toughest competition for years. We have a great rivalry going on with them and always get into heated battles on the ice. For years our sport was also like women's hockey

where Canada and U.S.A. dominated, but after the Paralympics in Sochi, Russia became a force to reckon with. Behind those two teams, Norway, Czech Republic, South Korea, and Italy are good matches to watch.

Q. What are your sticks made of?
Today, sledge hockey sticks are made of the same material as a typical composite stick. They have evolved from the one piece wooden sticks that were used in the beginning. Guys started cutting a carbon shaft open and insert a wooden blade. Carbon blades then appeared and today guys are working with one piece composite sticks. Warrior Hockey and Easton are the two most common manufacturers of sledge hockey sticks.

Q. How do you shoot?
Shooting is just like regular hockey, both in a snapshot and a wrist shot. It begins with placing the puck slightly parallel to the hips. As the puck is loaded, the player leans forward with his body and shoulder to twist the body by tightening the core to build up tension. During the release, the player can either let the puck roll from the heel to the toe and finish with a wrist shot, or he can snap the puck from the mid-point of the stick for a snap shot.

Q. How much do hockey sleds cost?
A sledge hockey sled will run between $600 - $850 depending on requirements. Beginners should buy an adjustable model in order to learn seating position, height, and blade width. Once this is figured out and the player knows they won't be adjusting anymore, then it's time to move up to a custom molded frame. Custom frames are $850 and it's a good idea to have a spare in case one gets bent. A 200lb + guy competing at the national level will find it common to bend a sled at least once a year.

Q. Is sledge hockey played full contact?
YES! Absolutely, one of the most exciting parts about our sport is that it is full contact, just like regular hockey. In sledge hockey you will notice a few differences. When we hit each other along the boards we don't have

the glass for give. The boards are solid. To really crush a player, line them up a foot or two off the wall and then hammer them through the air into the boards. It hurts! Second, because you need to line up a guy shoulder to shoulder, it can be tricky mid-ice. To catch a guy with his head down is good for lining them up. It also works well to pivot the hips sideways and essentially hip check a guy. It's tricky, but these skills pay off!

Q. Is there fighting in sledge hockey?
Because we play very few games a year, and we almost always play in tournaments, there aren't as many fights as we would like. If you fight and get suspended, you may be gone for the remainder of that game plus one more. Missing two out of five games sucks. However, that does not mean we don't get into battles! There's a ton of fighting that goes down near the crease. It's always good to get in a goalies face. Dropping the gloves in sledge though means we lose our sticks. We can't move around then, and to get a pick stabbed in the bare hand or have a fingertip run over by a sled blade, would end the player's career in a snap!

Q. How do you skate backwards?
In sledge hockey it's extremely difficult to skate backwards. You can do it, but it's slow and not practical for the speed of play. What you need to do is focus on playing the angles properly. Like stand up hockey, if you are playing a one on one situation you need to take away the middle of the ice and force the opponent to the outside. You also need to constantly make shoulder checks and adjust your speed so the guy doesn't blow by. Don't give him too much space on the rush. Close the gap and play accordingly.

Q. How do goalies play net?
Goalies will typically sit one of two ways. The cross-legged position has the player facing their chest straight forward. This position is common for single-legged amputees and enables very quick movement around the crease. It makes using the blocker and glove easier but opens the door for low shots on the ice. Option two would be sitting with legs in front

and then turning the body sideways to use the glove and blocker. This position covers the bottom of the net easier but makes crease movement more difficult. Currently both Team Canada goalies sit cross-legged.

Q. Do you have to be disabled to play sledge hockey?
At the national level players must have an impairment in the lower body to qualify for the Paralympics, Team Canada, and even the Development National Team. An impairment can be classified by balance, mobility, flexibility, coordination, and other methods which gauge a player's level of disability on a points scale.

At the house league level, anyone can play. Many club teams actually survive simply because able bodied players choose to join either to support a family member or a friend with a disability.

Q. What are some of the common disabilities on Sledge Team Canada?
Sledge Team Canada is comprised mostly of players with spina bifida, cerebral palsy, spinal cord injuries, and single-legged or double-legged amputees. For example, the majority of team USA is comprised of double-legged amputees.

Q. How do you get on and off the ice surface?
At a hockey rink that has been properly modified, the benches are removed where players usually sit and there is a hard plastic surface placed above the rubber to slide the sleds on. The ice surface should be flush with the door entry and players can slide into the bench and out. The plastic doesn't dull the blades and is fairly easy to move on. In the Paralympics ice was used instead of plastic, making the transition even smoother. Trainers or the backup goalie will usually operate the door for the players so the coaches can focus on the game.

Q. Are the rules the same in sledge hockey?
Yes, the rules are the same with one additional penalty, "T-boning". A T-bone is when a player collides with another player in a "T" direction, just

like an automobile accident. This is a minor infraction. Other penalties are the same though players rarely would get a tripping or hooking call. Common penalties are given for roughing, interference, and holding. Icing, offside, and face-offs are the same. Currently when playing under the IIHF rules we play fifteen minute periods. In Canada we are constantly working to bring the sport to twenty minute periods all the time.

Q. When was sledge hockey invented?
Sledge hockey was invented by three Swedish wheelchair athletes on a frozen lake in Stockholm in 1961. In 1976 a sled was brought home to Canada, and then in 1992 Sledge Hockey of Canada was born. In 1994, sledge hockey was introduced as a demonstration sport at the Paralympic Winter Games in Lillehammer, Norway. The sport has since become a full medal event at the Paralympic Winter Games. Canada has participated in sledge hockey in each of the Paralympic Winter Games. In 2004 sledge hockey came under the umbrella of Hockey Canada.

Q. What is a better advantage in the sport, having legs or being an amputee?
Personally, I think being a below the knee double-amputee or someone with spina bifida are at the highest advantage. It's a medium point between having legs and not. It's allows agility along with good size and weight. Whether one is, like me, 205lbs with two legs or has an above knee double amputation, each has its advantages and disadvantages. I work well hammering guys in corners, protecting the puck with my legs, and being a screen in front of the net. I have a harder time accelerating though and lack agility. A double amputee would likely have super fast acceleration and the ability to turn on a dime. They are harder to defend but easy to knock over.

Q. Do you have any tips or tricks you can share?
Well, regarding the sticks, I like to use baby powder over the edges of the blade to help avoid my stick sticking to the inside of my glove. Sometimes

you will see a guy over-skate a puck and it's simply because in that brief moment, there is a lapse where the blade gets stuck in their hand and a player can't get their hand down the shaft. This is because of the glue from the hockey tape. Some guys use wax or nothing at all. I need baby powder or wax. I can't use nothing at all. I also prefer a graphite shaft that is not sticky and my blades to be nearly slippery so I can have fast hands.

Q. Do you ever get stabbed with the end of the sticks?
Yes! Sometimes intentionally and sometimes unintentionally. Ironically I received my worst scars ever both times from my own stick getting jabbed into my rib cage during a hit. I had seven stitches the first game in my rib cage, then in the Sochi Paralympics I did it again. There is a level of respect in the game to not intentionally stab someone but it certainly has happened. I've done it. You better hope that when you do you don't get caught because you will be ejected.

Q. What's your training schedule like?
During the Paralympic year we go hard. That's when everything drops and we are a full time athlete. Preparing for Sochi I was training in the gym five days a week and getting on the ice three to five days a week, sometimes more. Sustaining that longer than one season is really hard when one still needs to earn a living and work a job. Other times of the year I try to hit the gym three to five times a week and to get two to three ice sessions in each week. Summer is a good time to bulk up and winter is when I work on conditioning.

Q. Where can I buy a sledge hockey sled?
Laurie Howlett of Unique Inventions in Peterborough, Ontario makes sleds for most people in the sport. Laurie provides people with disabilities high quality, affordable equipment. Laurie's shop has expanded over the years, and they manufacture all parts for their sled in-house and operate all year round. Worldwide shipping is available. He has sold sleds to other national teams including Sweden, Germany, and Czech Republic.

To have Kevin speak at your next event, please visit

www.kevinrempel.com

Let's Connect

Snapchat: remps_05
Twitter: @KevinRempel
Instagram: @KevinRempel
YouTube: YouTube.com/kevinrempel
Facebook: Facebook.com/rempelinspires

About the Author

■ ■ ■

Kevin's original dream was to ride motocross professionally, but after a career ending crash in 2006 left him paralyzed from the chest down, he was forced to find a new passion. Kevin played hockey as a kid, so when sledge hockey came into the picture it was a definite "yes" to pursue. After joining the team during the 2010 - 2011 season Kevin has helped Canada earn multiple medals including gold in the 2013 World Championships and bronze in the 2014 Paralympics in Sochi, Russia. Today Kevin focuses on sharing his story inspiring others to overcome their challenges, achieve their dreams, and help grow the sport of sledge hockey.

Made in the USA
Columbia, SC
13 September 2019